Lessons From The
Pioneers:

Reflections
Along The
Oregon Trail

Jay Mennenga

Potential Press
Burley, Idaho

Lessons From The Pioneers: Reflections Along The Oregon Trail.

Copyright c 1993 by Jay Mennenga.

First Printing 1993   Second Printing 1995

Second Printing edited by Mark Reisetter, Lewiston, Minnesota
Printed in the United States of America by Gilliland Printing, Inc., Arkansas City, Kansas
Cover Design by Rick Schuster, Sacco Schuster & Associates, Omaha, Nebraska

Unless otherwise stated, all Scripture quotes are taken from **The Living Bible** 1971. Used by permission of Tyndale House Publishers, Inc., Wheaton, IL 60189. All rights reserved. Excerpts, including diagrams, taken from **The 7 Habits of Highly Effective People**, COPYRIGHT 1989 by Stephen R. Covey. Reprinted by permission of Simon & Schuster, Inc. Excerpts, including maps, taken from the book: **Places Rated Almanac** by: Richard Boyer & David Savageau 1989. Used by permission of the publisher, Prentice Hall Travel/A division of Simon & Schuster, New York.

Dedicated To The

"Pioneer Spirit"

May It Be Part Of Our Lives

Today!

CONTENTS

DIAGRAMS AND MAPS

Pioneers recorded many accounts of their travels along the Oregon Trail. This book encourages you to do the same. Please write your reflections in the wide margins. May your "journey" be enriched as you follow the Trail. Have fun!

Jay L L Lemanya

PREFACE: HOW TO USE THIS BOOK

Welcome to the **Oregon Trail**! 1993 marked the **sesquicentennial** of the Great Migration to Oregon in 1843. There were many observances along the entire Trail commemorating this historic occasion. Over 150 years later, the lure of this Trail still draws modern-day pioneers.

You also selected a **unique** book! Besides learning from the pioneer journey, you will have the opportunity to reflect on your own metaphorical "journey" through life. You will notice this book has wide margins. This is for you to enter your reflections as you travel the Trail. You might even try sketching. You are encouraged to draw and write in this book - after you buy it, of course! The purpose of this book is to personalize your Oregon Trail odyssey. Let it come alive with adventure and meaning!

As a student of this important event in American history, you probably have a basic knowledge of the route and what the pioneers had to overcome to reach their goal in Oregon. You may have read or purchased several excellent guides to use when following the Trail. These books provide a map and description of the historic sites. Some books use pictures and paintings to help you visualize the scenes historically or as they appear today. Much use is made of pioneer diaries.

Several books present a more scholarly approach to this migration. One uses a historical perspective, tracing the use of the Trail from the discovery of America to its use by the emigrants. Another is a doctoral dissertation, utilizing anecdotes, letters and journal entries. The bibliography at the back of this book provides a list of these books, which I have read and used.

The above books are excellent in their historical treatment of the pioneer saga. However, they do not emphasize what we, as contemporary Oregon Trail travelers can **learn** from their experiences. This will be the thrust of my book. As such it will **complement** the other books written about the Oregon Trail.

Today we refer to the courage of the emigrants, the necessity of cultivating a pioneer spirit, together with their trials - not to be confused with trails! We discuss their search for the "good life" and the reasons why they decided to journey to Oregon. We use their journey as a metaphor for our own search for a better life. As the longest voluntary migration in American history, it is certainly worthy to travel, discuss and reflect on its importance.

This book is a series of **essays** relating selected experiences of the 1843 pioneer journey to our lives. Each chapter will provide the historical setting for that experience, based on my observations and pictures while traveling the Oregon Trail during the past seven summers.

Each chapter will focus on **one concept** important to their journey. By drawing from the fields of philosophy, psychology and religion, I will apply the emigrants' experiences to our own lives. I will attempt to answer questions relevant to our lives today. The **goal** of this book is to provide ideas that can enrich our lives 150 years later. The format of the book thus synthesizes the past with the present, the concrete with the abstract, in the style of Robert Pirsig's two best-sellers: **Zen and the Art of Motorcycle Maintenance** and **Lila**. This book includes a description of the route of the Oregon Trail, ten pioneer lessons for contemporary Americans, concluding with applications for our lives.

There are many lessons we can learn from this epic journey. For example, they first had to **decide whether to attempt this type of travel**. This entailed a fairly high degree of risk. What motives and reasons did they use to leave? What part did risk-taking and faith play? Are these the same motives and reasons we use to change our current situation today? To what degree are we risk-takers? How does faith relate to our decision making today?

Once this decision was made, the pioneers needed to know what **supplies** to take. This called for prioritization. Which goods were most essential? Which could be left at home? Today how do we determine what to purchase? How do we distinguish between needs and wants?

Since the early emigrants were venturing into mainly uncharted territory in 1843, they needed **guides and guidebooks**. How important were maps to them? How reliable were these instruments? When should they deviate from the main route to take cutoffs? In today's information age, how do we determine what sources are reliable? What is our "guidance system?" When do we know when to follow the main road or take the "road less traveled?"

The pioneers tried to follow **rivers** to acquire the basic necessities of water, wood and grass. Without these three ingredients, the journey would have failed. How important are these resources in today's West? What are the basics we need today? How are they provided? What other needs do we have today?

Forts and missions were welcome stopping points along the Trail. They provided supplies, protection and places of rest along the way. How important to us are modern "forts and missions?" What type of protection do we need today? How important is rest and relaxation?

Landmarks along the Trail served - not only as guides - but as sources of inspiration and a break in the monotony of travel. How important are landmarks in our personal journey? What causes or ideas inspire us today? How important are the aesthetic aspects of Nature to us today? When is something "totally awesome?"

The emigrants needed to be aware of the **changing weather conditions**, since they had little protection when traveling. They experienced the whole gamut of Nature's fury and learned a healthy respect for the skies. How important are weather-related events to us today? How do we protect ourselves from these phenomena today? Do these events cause us to "look up" and respect Nature's God?

The pioneers traveled in wagon trains, composed mainly of **family units and friends**. Even though there were quarrels and irritations, they needed to cooperate and depend upon each other to successfully complete their journey. Indians, though strangers, were generally friendly and provided needed guidance and material assistance. How important are our family units and friends to us today? How do we work together with family and friends to accomplish personal and career goals? What needs are provided by these interactions? What kind of attitude do we have toward Indians and strangers in today's society?

During the long journey, a **division of responsibility** existed among the men, women and children. Each knew their **skills and abilities** and performing them was essential to making daily progress. These tasks required a high degree of discipline for their successful completion. Does a division of labor exist in our society today or are the roles blurred? How do we assess our God-given talents? How do we discipline ourselves in the use of our time and talents today?

The emigrants encountered many **obstacles** throughout their nearly six months and 2,000 miles of traveling. In spite of enduring everything from natural to human trials, they kept going. What resources did they call upon to continue their journey? How do we cope with personal and societal problems today? Are the pioneer resources the same ones we use in overcoming obstacles today? What are the components composing individual character?

Finally, the pioneers **achieved their goal** and found their "good life" in Oregon. The arduous journey was successful for approximately 90% of those who started. They were finally able to reach their potential in the Willamette River Valley. They no doubt felt a great deal of satisfaction in reaching the "promised land." What types of goals do we accomplish? How do we measure success today? How can we reach our potential? What types of activities and/or experiences give us satisfaction and meaning today?

The "baby boomers" and "yuppies" looked for answers to the above questions through the acquisition of material goods, career advancement and social status. Today, this same age group - those born from 1946-1964 - is changing from the "me" generation of the 1980s to the "we" generation of the 1990s. The emphasis has shifted from "having" to "becoming." The Biblical admonition "life does not consist in the abundance of things"(Luke 12:15) is becoming more important as they search for lasting satisfaction and meaning in life.

As you can see, this journey will require some "soul-searching" on your part. Since most of the Oregon Trail is through sparsely-populated areas, your traveling time should allow for personal reflection. So, if you like reading and learning about the pioneers, "are a baby-boomer" or older, and are willing to apply the emigrant experiences to your life, keep traveling. "Happy trail to you!"

Route of the Oregon Trail

Map 1

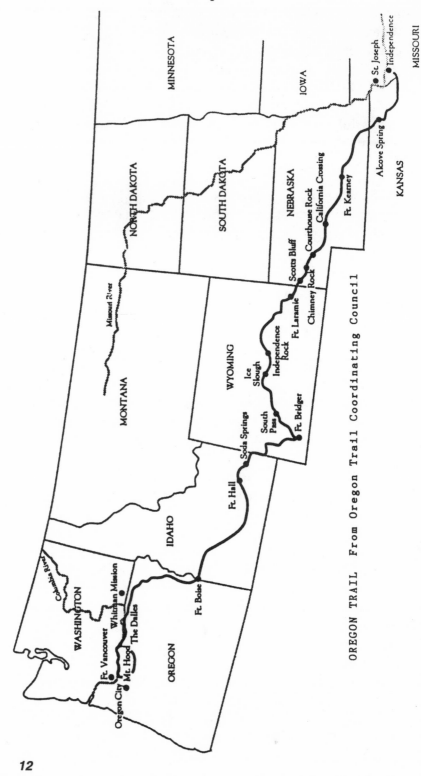

OREGON TRAIL From Oregon Trail Coordinating Council

12

INTRODUCTION

The Journey Begins

The year was 1843. Some families in the Midwest were restless. Economic conditions on the the farm were poor. The Depression of 1837 drastically reduced prices. More settlers from the East were locating in the Midwest, creating overcrowding with neighbors as close as 12 miles! These families were tired of the same routine and yearned for a change.

At the same time, fur traders and mountain men were heading West in search of adventure and animal pelts. Missionaries, spreading the Gospel to the Indians, also came back and told stories about their explorations. This created an excitement and an expectation of a "better life" elsewhere.

The most common destination of these travelers was Oregon. It was described as a land of opportunity, where farmers were promised free land in return for settling there. Natural resources, such as fertile land and abundant moisture in the Willamette Valley, would produce bumper crops. Trees, fruits and fish also flourished. The climate was proclaimed as being more healthful and moderate than the Midwest. No frigid winters with snow, nor sweltering and stormy summers. Oregon was portrayed as the place where the "good life" could be obtained.

As a result over 50,000 pioneers made the long 2,000 mile journey from Missouri to Oregon from 1840-1859. [1] This movement along the Oregon Trail became the longest voluntary mass migration in the history of the United States. Despite facing disease, shortages of fresh food and water, accidents, animal losses, thunderstorms, intense heat, blizzards, unfriendly Indians and boredom on the Trail, over 90% of those who started reached their destination. Not content with the status quo at home, these "risk-takers" found their perception of the "good life" in Oregon.

These pioneers sacrificed much to make this journey. They left their relatives and friends back home. Some of the men departed without their families, returning for them later. Most of the possessions in their homes - particularly the bulky pieces of furniture - could not fit into their covered wagons. Consequently, they had to prioritize which goods should be taken. Many of these items did not complete the journey, since the oxen tired from pulling these heavy loads. These pieces were simply abandoned on the Trail, to be picked up by someone else.

Instead they took practical items, such as food, tools and firearms. The food had to be preserved without refrigeration. Water, firewood or buffalo chips for cooking was gathered on the journey. Grass had to be obtained for the oxen, mules, horses and cattle. The tools were used for repairs on the wagons. Firearms and ammunition were used for protection against unfriendly Indians and wild animals. These weapons were also needed to hunt buffalo, deer, antelope and other game animals.

Their wealth consisted of the possessions they took with them, including any cash. Anything else was left back in civilization. Thus their assets needed to be mobile, so they could be put to use in Oregon.

What kind of person and family would give up their

familiar surroundings, immobile wealth and family and friends to face an unknown journey of 2,000 miles to a "promised land" they hadn't seen? They had to be risk-takers, confident they would complete their journey. From where did this confidence come? They must have had faith God would protect and guide them to their chosen destination.

The long trip required specific skills of the pioneers. A division of labor existed among the men, women and children. The men, using their mechanical aptitude, were responsible for repairing the wagons, determining the route and the nightly campsites and providing protection from Indians, robbers and animals. The women, using their domestic skills, did the cooking, set up and broke camp, and mended clothing. The children were responsible for gathering firewood, and feeding and caring for the animals. To successfully complete each task required specific knowledge and know-how.

In spite of the many natural obstacles and duties while traveling, these pioneers still took time to enjoy the aesthetic pleasures of the journey. On most evenings they would socialize by singing and "fiddling" around the campfire. They would also enjoy the beautiful sunsets. By arising at dawn, they could enjoy the beautiful sun throughout the day.

While traveling they had plenty of time to enjoy the splendid scenery. Even though much of the journey became monotonous after miles of treeless prairie, certain natural features(Chimney Rock and Independence Rock) stood out to provide variety. Unique rock formations, mountains, trees and rivers added color to their travels. The emigrants also experienced the awesomeness of Nature, with its duststorms, thunderstorms, searing heat and early snowstorms.

Format Of The Book

This book is not only an historical account of the pioneers' quest for their "good life" in Oregon, but also(and more importantly) their saga contains lessons for us today. There is much we can learn about our own lives by studying the experiences of these adventuresome pioneers. Whether or not we realize it, we are all on a journey to find a more enriching and satisfying life. Thus the concrete travel of these emigrants serves as a **metaphor** to describe the more abstract "journey" on which we have embarked.

The book focuses on the pioneer journey in 1843. This was the year the first significant wagon train completed the trek from Missouri to Oregon. This epic journey is known as the Great Emigration.

Why Read This Book?

You may be asking, "What type of interests should I possess to read this book?" **First**, you should be willing to engage in **reflective thinking.** You need to look "inside yourself" to evaluate your life vis-a-vis the pioneer experiences.

Second, you should have an interest in **history** - specifically the Oregon Trail. Maybe you have read books and diaries about the pioneers. Perhaps you have even followed portions of the original Trail. The basis for these essays comes from my five summers of traveling this Trail.

Third, you should have an interest in reading and discussing **ideas**. One of my favorite sayings is:

"Great minds think about ideas;
Average minds think about people;
Small minds think about things."

While this book deals with ideas, people and things, the emphasis is on ideas. To receive maximum benefit from reading and reflecting on this book, you need to be a great mind. That doesn't mean you need a college degree in philosophy - only that you have an interest in ideas.

Fourth, since I draw from the areas of philosophy,

psychology and religion, you should believe that the works of Aristotle, Abraham Maslow, together with teachings from the Bible, are important sources for learning about living meaningful lives today.

If you share these four interests with me, read on! We'll travel with the pioneers as we learn from their experiences. After all, don't you learn more about life by enjoying the trip rather than hurrying to reach your destination? Relax and come with me along our "journey."

Where The Trail Ran

Those of you who have purchased trail maps may skip this section. For the rest of you, I will provide an overview of the main trail from its starting point in Independence, Missouri to its end in Oregon City, Oregon. Although this route encompassed 1932 miles through seven states, there were many deviations and shortcuts from the main trail. I will only describe the most traveled route.

The emigrants usually followed rivers, since they were a source of water for drinking, grass for the animals and firewood for cooking. The lowest elevation and most level topography was generally along these rivers.

Around the middle of May, the pioneers left Independence, Missouri, the most popular starting point. The route traveled northwest through northeast Kansas, following the Kansas and Little Blue Rivers. Several springs(Alcove, Big and Vermillion) provided special resting places.

Crossing into southeast Nebraska, they followed the Little Blue River until it emptied into the Platte River near present Kearney. Fort Kearny - a different spelling than the city - was the first outpost to provide supplies after 325 miles on the Trail. The Platte and North Platte Rivers were important to the pioneers through Nebraska(most of this route closely parallels today's Interstate 80). The wagons gradually gained elevation from 800 to almost 4,000 feet above sea level at Scottsbluff. Western Nebraska provided the first glimpses of a more rugged terrain with Windlass Hill and several looming landmarks(Courthouse Rock, Jail Rock, Chimney Rock and Scotts Bluff).

Crossing into Wyoming the emigrants first saw Laramie Peak, which they mistook for the Rocky Mountains. They enjoyed a taste of eastern civilization at Fort Laramie, 650 miles from Independence. This fort was an important oasis along the Trail. Continuing their northwesterly direction along the North Platte River, the pioneers rested at Ayers Natural Bridge and resupplied their livestock and themselves at Fort Caspar, 800 miles along the way.

The route then switched southwesterly along the Sweetwater River. The pioneers tried to reach Independence Rock, another important landmark, around the 4th of July. Devil's Gate and Split Rock - both aptly named - were reached before South Pass, 900 miles from Independence. This shallow pass(7,500 feet elevation) across the Continental Divide was easily crossed. Because South Pass marked the emigrants' arrival to the frontier at the halfway point, it was symbolically the most important landmark.

Even though several cutoffs over dry ground saved miles, most pioneers chose the safer route to Ft. Bridger, over 1,000 miles from the starting point. From this fort the route again veered northwesterly through the green Bear River Valley to Ft. Hall near Pocatello, Idaho, 1200 miles from Independence. For the next 300 miles the Snake River provided the essentials of life for the pioneers as they traveled to Ft. Boise(1,500 miles out) and through Idaho into the "promised land" of Oregon. Traveling Interstate 84 today will parallel the original Trail through Idaho and Oregon.

After leaving the Snake River at Farewell Bend, the pioneers came over Flagstaff Hill near Baker. There they first saw the green trees of the Blue Mountains - what a refreshing view this must have been! However, they still had over 300 tough traveling miles to go, including the traversing of these mountains. The Whitman Mission in Washington furnished the last respite before most emigrants floated down the wide Columbia River to Oregon City, 1932 miles and five and one half months from Independence.

From this point the pioneers fanned south through the rich Willamette River Valley in search of fertile land to grow crops and abundant wood to build homes for their families. This long and arduous trip was worth the effort for most of those successfully completing the journey. We can learn much from this important historical and human event.

The Author And The Trail

For the past seven summers I have traveled on or close to the Oregon Trail, stopping at every major historical site described above. I followed the original Trail as closely as possible while staying mainly on hard-surfaced roads. Occasionally I ventured on dirt roads as far as my low-clearance automobile would allow(I recommend a high-clearance vehicle for this type of exploration). I found Haines' **Historic Sites Along THE OREGON TRAIL** particularly useful in locating and describing sites. I also found state highway maps valuable guides.

I traveled by myself - unlike the pioneer families in their wagon trains. I camped in a tent - like the emigrants. I found a campsite when the sun started to set in the West - like the pioneers. I brought my food and fixed it myself, or ate in restaurants. I killed no buffalo and caught no fish - unlike the pioneers. I was never attacked by unfriendly Indians - like the majority of emigrants. As you can see, I wasn't completely authentic. Maybe next time I'll take a covered wagon!

While driving I compared my journey to the Great Migration of 1843. I attempted to empathize with the pioneer situations. The insights gained from these trips provide the basis for the rest of this book.

Meanwhile, back in Independence, those gathered had obviously made the important decision to forge ahead to Oregon. What were their motives and reasons? What part did risk-taking and faith play? How can their experiences benefit us as we face major decisions in our lives? That's the subject for our first lesson. Westward Ho!

Lesson One

RISK-TAKING: THE DECISION TO TRAVEL TO OREGON

Setting

You're living on a farm in the Midwest in 1836. Previous to this time you were fairly prosperous, with good crops and an adequate income to provide a comfortable life for your family. Then the Panic of 1837 hit, depressing farm prices and threatening your standard of living. All the while more people are moving from the East to the Midwest, creating closer neighbors and less new land.

For the next six years reports of a better life in Oregon drift eastward. Reports of fertile land for bountiful harvests, huge trees for building houses and clear streams for providing fish are brought back by trappers and missionaries. The climate was described as mild without the extremes of the summer heat and winter cold. Diseases, such as malaria and cholera, prevalent in the Midwest, were unknown. There was room to stake your claim without intrusion by neighbors.

You also hear reports of the distant conflict between England and the United States over disputed land in the Northwest. Because of the influence of the Hudson Bay Company, the English claimed much of Canada and the Northwest Territory. Would more Americans traveling to Oregon save this area for America? Do we have a patriotic duty to fight England again?

Some of your neighbors are becoming restless with these reports. Is the "grass really greener on the other side of the country?" Was the spirit of adventure and the frontier spirit calling some? Or is a "bird in the hand(at home) worth two in the bush?"(in Oregon) Should we give up the security and familiarity of our present situation to risk the possibility of a "better life" in an unknown land? Are we willing to leave our relatives and friends for this journey?

What's a family to do?

These families in 1843 faced a major decision - to move or stay? This decision is similar to those faced by many Americans today living in our mobile society. Today's moves are generally motivated by career changes. These changes usually lead to geographic moves.

Just like the pioneers of the 1840s, Americans 150 years later are still moving west. According to John Naisbitt's best-selling **Megatrends**, the 1980 census revealed that, for the first time in American history, more Americans are living in the South and West than in the East and North. **2** The 1990 census continues this trend, which Naisbitt says is irreversible in our lifetimes. **3** This latest census reveals 56% of Americans living in the South and West. **4** Americans are migrating westward toward the land of opportunity. **5**

The pioneers were probably not aware of nationwide trends like those listed above. The nation was gradually moving from the East coast to the Midwest. However, in 1843 no one could visualize how far west the population center would move in the next 20 years.

Decision-Making Factors

How did these pioneer families make the big decision? What criteria did they use? Did the father write down the pros and cons on a yellow legal pad - if they had them then? Did he then call a family meeting to discuss these points? After praying about the decision, was a vote then taken, giving every family member an equal voice or were more votes given to the adults than the children? Did the majority rule, or did the "head" of the household decide? What if the mother didn't agree with the decision? What if the children didn't agree? How was the decision finally resolved? Was a compromise solution negotiated? Did some family members move while others stayed? Did the father move and come back for his family after establishing a home in Oregon?

We can only speculate as to how this decision was determined by the pioneer families. We do know several factors that may have influenced their decisions. First, the families were more traditional than those of today. Therefore, what the father decided was usually what was done. With wives mainly working at home - without an independent source of income - they had little choice but to follow their husbands west.

Second, the decision was probably influenced by how much of a "risk-taker" the decision-maker was. Some people are more willing to try new experiences. Others prefer a more secure environment, reflecting the status quo. A person's willingness to change could be depicted on a continuum as follows:

Degree of Willingness To Change

10	5	0
High	Moderate	Low

Those persons making the decision to travel to Oregon could probably be placed on the high side(7-10) side of the above continuum. Those remaining at home would probably merit a ranking of 0-3.

Application: When you are confronting a possible move, where would you place yourself on the above scale? ___ Are you more of a "risk-taker" or a "status-quoer?" What makes a person one or the other?

A person may be experiencing a "bad" situation, but still be reluctant to change. Conversely, a family may have everything "going their way" but still decide to change their environment. Why?

There are several possible reasons to explain the above seeming paradoxes. First, I believe a person's self-concept is related to a willingness to change. A person who (1) knows he has certain God-given gifts and talents and (2) is confident they can be applied in a new situation will be more willing to venture into the unknown. On the other hand, a person feeling unsure of her abilities is less likely to try new experiences. A person's level of self-concept could be depicted on the following continuum as:

Degree of Self-Concept

10	5	0
High	Moderate	Low

Application How do you rank yourself as to degree of self-concept? ___

Thus a person with a high degree of self-concept(7-10) would be more willing to take risks. It would also follow that a person possessing a low degree of self-concept(0-3) would be more apt to prefer the status quo. Those persons in 1843 who decided to journey to Oregon would probably score high on this continuum, while those choosing to stay would score low.

Therefore, by relating the two above continuums, I am correlating a high degree of risk with a high degree of self-concept, and a low degree of risk with a low degree of self-concept. There are obviously exceptions to the above conclusions. Remember, this is not an empirical study, but only the common sense conclusions of the author.

Related to the concepts of risk-taking and self-concept as factors in making decisions is the element of faith. Risk is an inherent component of faith. In both cases a person is willing to start on a journey without knowing the territory and the final destination. Certainly this was the case with the pioneers. The greater their risk, the stronger their faith.

An example of the importance of faith was evidenced by the Biblical character Abraham. When God called him to leave his country, "he went out, not knowing where he was going." 6 Abraham and his wife Sarah didn't analyze the pros and cons, nor wait for "things to fall into place" before making their decision. They left promptly and willingly, convinced that God's direction for them was in their best interests. They were certainly a pioneer family.

How does the example of Abraham relate to the emigrants and us today? How important is faith in making decisions? Charles Swindoll, in **Abraham: A Model Of Pioneer Faith**, poses the question, ". . how can we know if He(God) is prompting us to move into new and unfamiliar territory?" 7 Swindoll posits five factors to consider.

First, "there is an increasing uneasiness with our current situation." 8 The Panic of 1837 no doubt contributed to an uneasiness for pioneer families. Some were also adventurous and restless, ready to move on to new frontiers - literally. Is there an uneasiness about your present family situation or career prospects prompting a possible change?

Second, "there is also a heightening level of curiosity regarding a new challenge." **9** Glowing reports of the "good life" in Oregon caused many Midwestern families to want to learn more about this "promised land." Are you interested in learning more about new opportunities elsewhere?

Third, the importance of attachments to security, material comforts and the familiar become less important. **10** The pioneer families were willing to leave most of their possessions at home - including their home - and only travel with the essentials(more on this in the next chapter). In our affluent surroundings, are you willing to reduce your standard of living for the promise of a higher standard later, or possibly a permanent reduction? Are you willing to leave family and friends for a new venture? Are you willing to change your surroundings for a new environment?

Fourth, the "desire to obey God at any cost eclipses all other desires." **11** Some of the pioneers journeyed West because of "Manifest Destiny." This term was used to justify America's claim to Oregon as "our manifest destiny to overspread and possess as the whole of the continent which Providence has given us for the great experiment of liberty and federated self-government." **12** These emigrants saw it as their mission to travel into uncharted lands to obey God and assist the United States in its dispute with England. Their journey was part of a larger plan with a purpose. It became their mission.

Finding Your Mission In Life

Do you believe God has a mission in life for you? If so, (a) how do you find it and (b) what is it? Richard Bolles, in one of the appendices to his best-selling **What Color Is Your Parachute?**, uses a spiritual approach in answering this question. He delineates the three stages of our mission in the following order:

1. To find the source of your mission. This can best be done by constant communication with God.

2. To do daily what you can to make this world a better place to live. You will find these tasks by the leading of God's Spirit within you.

3. To utilize your God-given gifts and talents which you most enjoy:

    (a) in the setting(s) most appealing to you,

        and

    (b) for the purpose which God needs to have done in this world. **13**

Bolles sees the first two stages as ones we share with the human race, with the third stage being uniquely ours. However, before we can discover our interests, gifts and talents, we must be participating in the first two stages. If we aren't faithful in the little things, how can we expect to be given greater responsibilities? **14** Bolles concludes that our mission should intersect with (1) the kind of work that you need most to do and (2) the world needs most to have done. **15** I highly recommend reading Bolles' entire appendix - and book - for shedding additional light on this important topic.

Vision, Mission and Passion

Two concepts related to mission are vision and passion. A person with a vision creates a picture of a probable outcome. The emigrants saw their "good life" in Oregon before beginning their journey. Glowing reports from early trappers and missionaries contributed to this positive view.

Three sources illustrate the importance of vision. The prophet Isaiah states the consequences of a lack of vision: "Without a vision the people perish." Viktor Frankl, a Jewish psychiatrist who spent time in a German concentration camp during World War II, explained why some prisoners survived and others died - even though both groups possessed relatively good health. In his **Man's Search for Mean**

ing, Frankl concluded the survivors felt they had something significant to accomplish upon their release. It may have been being a father to his children or finishing a book(as did Frankl). Joel Barker, in his video "The Power of Vision", concludes with the following quotation:

> "Vision without action is only dreaming;
> Action without vision is only passing time;
> Vision plus action can change the world."

Once you see the vision you can formulate your mission - a more specific goal. The third ingredient needed is passion - an intense interest in an activity and the determination to complete it. The pioneers needed all three to successfully find their "good life" in Oregon.

Application Do we possess a vision, mission and passion for accomplishing our tasks today?

Back to faith and the pioneers. Finally, Swindoll sees the recurring thoughts of moving as evidence we are ready to "take the plunge" into new territory. **16** Before beginning their journey, the pioneers were probably thinking about the implications of their move. This enabled them to get mentally ready for the journey. Maybe you have or are currently experiencing these thoughts about an impending move. Hopefully the above factors will assist you in making your decision.

"Interpretive Center, Baker, OR"

SUPPLIES: KNOWING WHAT TO TAKE

Full speed ahead to Oregon! The tough decision has been made. Now comes the preparation time. More questions arise. What to take? How much of each good? What to do with the belongings we are leaving home? Did they have garage - or barn - sales then?

The goal of this preparation was to select supplies conducive to traveling in a ten by four foot canvas-covered wagon. This obviously called for prioritization. The two general types of supplies were those needed for (1) the journey and (2) in Oregon. Thus the emigrants needed both short and long term plans of action. Since there were few supply stations along the way(forts and missions), they may have been more concerned with the immediate supplies instead of those they wouldn't need for five months. If the pioneers forgot something at home, they couldn't just take the next interstate exit and buy their supplies along the way - like we can today.

Maslow's Hierarchy of Needs

Do we have this same tendency - to be more concerned with the present than the future, with today than to-morrow, with immediate rather than long-term goals? If so, why? According to Abraham Maslow's Hierarchy of Needs, satisfying the lower level needs(food, water, shelter, clothing and safety) takes precedence over the higher level needs of belonging and love, self-esteem, self-actualization, knowledge, understanding and the aesthetic.(see Diagram 1) Only as these concrete lower level needs are satisfied can a person concentrate on more abstract concerns; i.e., trying to reach your potential. The emigrants first needed to concentrate on the supplies that would ensure a safe arrival in Oregon before they could attempt to reach their potential there. Maslow's theory would seem to be true for the emigrants and us today. I will be referring to this important theory throughout the book.

Diagram 1.

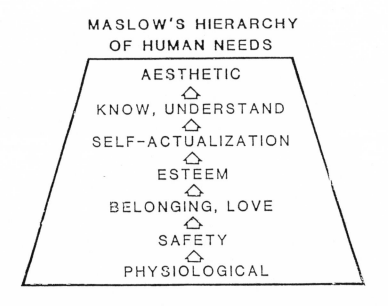

MASLOW'S HIERARCHY
OF HUMAN NEEDS

AESTHETIC

KNOW, UNDERSTAND

SELF-ACTUALIZATION

ESTEEM

BELONGING, LOVE

SAFETY

PHYSIOLOGICAL

Supplies For The Journey

Supplies for the journey included the following: (1)

wagon and tents (2) livestock (3) food and (4) miscellaneous items. The wagons needed to be simple, strong, and light, made from well-seasoned wood. The dry wood for the wheels would then be less susceptible to shrinking in the Western arid climate. The canvas covering was a double thickness and waterproofed. The wagon was high enough so a person could stand upright and walk down the center. The goods were packed on either side, providing a walkway down the middle for easier access. In order to carry the maximum amount of goods, the people usually slept outside in tents. Most of the time they walked to avoid the lurching and bumpy ride. Can you imagine walking 2,000 miles today? Usually only the sick or injured rode inside.

The most important livestock were those pulling the wagons. A great debate ensued among the fitness of horses, mules or oxen. Even though more expensive, mules were faster and endured the heat better. However, they lived up - or down - to their reputation of stubbornness! Oxen were less expensive and slower, but had more endurance. Most wagon trains preferred the oxen. Even though you some-times see pictures of wagons pulled by horses, they were a rarity. They lacked endurance and were a prime target for thievery by the Indians.

Do we consider similar factors when purchasing our main form of transportation(automobiles) today? Initial cost, whether a plain or luxury model, is a major consideration. Operating costs, including repairs and gas mileage, may also be important. Endurance, as reflected in how long the car will last, presents a third consideration. These factors were important to the pioneers, as they are to us when we choose transportation.

In making the above decision, the pioneers relied on "word of mouth" and guidebooks. There were not sources rating horses, mules and oxen according to the above crite-ria. In today's information age, we have a plethora of rating books, such as **Consumer Reports,** to assist us in choosing an automobile. However, recommendations from others is still important, as it was 150 years ago.

Since the pioneers could not count on hunting and fishing to supply most of their food along the trail, they brought most of their provisions. Captain Marcy's **The Prairie Traveler** recommended the following amounts for each adult:

150 pounds of flour or hard bread
25 pounds of bacon or pork
15 pounds of coffee
25 pounds of sugar
seasonings such as salt and pepper **17**

Other provisions included dried fruit to prevent scurvy - a disease caused by the lack of fresh fruit. Cattle and goats were taken as sources of milk and butter. Cages of chickens provided eggs. Once on the plains, the buffalo would furnish the main meat dish. Along the rivers, catfish, trout and salmon were the main catches.

Does this sound like a balanced diet for five months on the trail? Did they eat from the four basic food groups every day? Probably not. It was basic, but monotonous. No fast food places! No pizza! But they still survived on these provisions.

Other items needed for the journey included clothes, cooking utensils, tools for repairing the road and wagons, chains and ropes for the animals and wagons, groundcloths to prevent moisture from getting under tents at night, firearms for hunting and protection from Indians and robbers, medicines, religious books - including a Bible - and a fiddle for singing and relaxing at night.

Books and the fiddle were the only supplies not directly relating to satisfying Maslow's lower level needs(refer to Diagram 1). Singing around the campfire provided for belonging needs and would probably enhance the self-esteem of the player - if he hit the right notes! This music would also appeal to the aesthetic level of the participants. The books assisted in satisfying the need for knowledge and un-

derstanding.
Supplies For Oregon

The other type of supplies were those intended for use in Oregon. Among them were farming implements, tools for building houses and household furniture. The tools were considered lighter and more essential than the furniture. How many of the latter items to take became questionable. Should heavy keepsake items such as china cabinets, hutches, dining room tables and chairs and beds be taken? What about packing cast-iron cooking stoves? How did they decide? Once again decisions had to be made.

Aristotle's Real And Apparent Goods

These pioneer families were dealing with two types of goods. According to the philosopher Aristotle, there are two types of goods - real and apparent. Mortimer Adler, who interprets Aristotle's views in **Aristotle For Everybody: Difficult Thought Made Easy**, explains the differences. Real goods are similar to Maslow's needs - things that are inherently good for you. These goods can be further divided into limited and unlimited goods. The physical goods(food, clothes and shelter) are considered limited and should be acquired in moderation. You can eat, drink and sleep too much, buy too many clothes and spend too much on an elaborate house. However, the pursuit of knowledge and understanding, together with the enjoyment of aesthetic pleasures, can be unlimited. You can never have too many of them.

Aristotle's limited and unlimited real goods are closely related to Maslow's Hierarchy of Needs. Diagram 2 takes Maslow's Hierarchy(Diagram 1) and divides it into lower and higher level needs. These needs correspond to Aritstole's limited and unlimited real goods, respectively.

Diagram 2.

ARISTOTLE'S UNLIMITED AND LIMITED REAL GOODS

Unlimited Real Goods

Pleasures of the Mind

Goods of the Mind

Self-esteem and Honor

Friendship

Limited Real Goods

Wealth

Physical Goods

Diagram 2

Created by Jay Mennenga, revised by Ken Discher, Grimes, Iowa

Apparent goods are like wants - things we desire but don't really need. You can possess too many apparent goods. How the emigrants and we deal with apparent goods is crucial to our finding the "good life."

What does Aristotle have to say to these pioneers about their supplies? Their essential supplies would be the real goods - both needed and good for them on the journey and in Oregon. These would include everything they took except their heavy keepsakes. The latter furniture would be considered apparent goods - desired but not needed.

Paradoxically, we can desire the apparent goods that are not good for us while ignoring the real goods we need. This sounds like the dilemma faced by the Apostle Paul when he states, "The good I want to do I do not, but the evil I do not wish to do, that I do." **18** Paul's way out was through the power of Christ to make "the good. . . desirable and the desirable. . . good, as Aristotle would say. **19**

Aristotle sees the "good life" as acquiring all the real

goods we really need. Adler explains: "... the best plan of all... is one that aims at every real good in the right order and measure and, in addition, allows us to seek things we want but do not need[apparent goods], so long as getting them does not interfere with our being able to satisfy our needs or fulfill our capacities." **20**

Even though Aristotle sees real goods in the right order as the best plan for acquiring the "good life," this life can still be lived by acquiring some apparent goods. The proviso is that the latter goods cannot interfere with the acquisition of the former.

Pioneer Real and Apparent Goods

As applied to the emigrants' supplies, taking the heavy keepsakes(apparent goods) would be contributing to the "good life," if the rest of the goods(which were real) could still be included in the wagons. Even though the pioneers were probably not thinking of Aristotle when deciding what to take to Oregon, they understood essential and nonessential goods, and decided which to bring accordingly. Since most of their goods were real and not apparent, the only decisions involved which heavy furniture items, if any, to take.

Even though some families started the journey with apparent goods, they abandoned some of them as the conditions worsened. As the oxen tired of pulling the heavy loads, this furniture was jettisoned by the road. Passing wagons could see valuable pieces of furniture and stoves left to decay, or for others to pick up. These pioneers didn't even sell them but may have scratched a sign saying, "Free! Help yourself - if you can handle it." This "littering of the desert" allowed them to place more emphasis upon their real goods. Aristotle would have been proud of them! However, the environmentalists today would not have approved of "the greatest litterbugs in American history."

Contemporary Real and Apparent Goods

Today we have many more goods - real and apparent - than the emigrants. We spend more on the basic necessities of food, medicine, clothing, housing and transportation. The higher a family's income, the greater percentage is spent on Maslow's higher level needs. More is spent on books, television and video equipment, entertainment and cultural and recreational opportunities in pursuit of knowledge, understanding and the aesthetic. Our standard of living is much higher. We possess more wealth - both tangible(houses, furniture, cars) and intangible(investments).

With more choices in spending today, how can we follow Aristotle's prescription for leading the "good life"?(see Adler's quote #20) Do all families have to spend the same amounts for the same goods? How much should we spend on limited real goods? How do we distinguish between needs(real goods) and wants(apparent goods)? Can we determine certain goods to be real and others apparent for everyone?

Aristotle realizes that the spending habits may be different for different persons, even though they are following his formula for happiness. This is because individuals have different tastes for apparent goods over and above the acquisition of real goods. "Different things appear good to different people." 21 What one person wants may be an apparent good that doesn't hinder her pursuit of happiness and the "good life."

Applying Aristotle Today: Use Of Our Money

How can the economic middle and upper class contemporary Americans apply Aristotle's abstract principles to our concrete spending habits? Since these families possess more discretionary income than the pioneers, we have many spending choices. Since economic lower class persons generally spend more of their income on the basic necessities, their dilemma is more of survival than of choices. They aren't as concerned with apparent goods.

Let's begin with spending for limited real goods such

as food, clothing and shelter. Remember Aristotle warned you can spend too much on these items if this means you have little money left to enjoy the unlimited real goods of pursuing knowledge and enjoying the aesthetic beauty.

When shopping for **food** should we buy the least expensive items in each basic food group? For example, should we buy hamburger instead of steak, white instead of whole wheat bread, store brand instead of brand name milk, bananas instead of strawberries, generic instead of brand name corn? Or should we concentrate on the most nutritional value, regardless of the cost? These are decisions we make every day, probably without much thought.

When purchasing **clothes** should we shop at discount outlets for the best "deal," or prefer brand name items at well known stores? How many shoes, shirts, blouses, slacks, jeans, or suits do we need - a change of clothes for each day of the working week or each day of the month? How many seasonal clothes(shorts, coats) should be in our wardrobe? How much of each type of clothes can we afford?

Probably the most expensive single purchase we will make is our **house and furniture**. How do we determine how many square feet of living space we should utilize? How many rooms should our family enjoy? What quality of furniture should we use? Should this house have a three car attached garage for our vehicles? How large of a monthly payment can we afford?

With the exception of using a standardized formula to figure a house payment, the above questions do not have clear cut answers. If you use a budget you probably have spending guidelines for the above categories. A budget will assist you in saving money to spend on unlimited real goods.

What if you don't prepare and adhere to a budget? There is a tendency to waste money that could be better spent on more important items(unlimited real goods). What if you spend more money on food, clothing and shelter than you need, thereby neglecting certain cultural experiences that could enhance your knowledge and appreciation for aesthetic beauty?

Aristotle would conclude your spending for apparent goods(the desires above your needs) has interfered with the acquisition of the unlimited real goods, thereby preventing you from living the "good life." Conversely, he would determine it would be acceptable to spend this excess money on limited real goods if it did **not** interfere with the pursuit of the higher goods. The higher your income, the more you can spend on apparent goods without interfering with unlimited real goods. Therefore the question is not how much money you spend on each type of good, but the impact this allocation of funds has on pursuing unlimited real goods.

Applying Aristotle Today: Use Of Our Time

So far I have only been depicting limited and unlimited goods in terms of spending habits. Maslow's higher level needs can be enjoyed apart from monetary concerns. Enjoying family and friends(belonging, love), developing a positive self-concept(esteem), reaching your potential(self-actualization), learning(knowing, understanding) and enjoying the arts and Nature(aesthetic) require more quality time than money in most instances. Thus the stewardship of our time is as important as wise use of our money. As the Psalmist expresses: "Teach us to number our days and recognize how few they are; help us to spend them as we should." **22**

Even though the pioneers were preoccupied with satisfying their basic needs, they still made time to sing, fiddle and socialize around the campfire. Many found time to read and write in their diaries, recording their experiences, from which we can learn today. Their schedules were not as busy as ours. I bet they didn't even use Franklin planners!

If the emigrants found time to enjoy the unlimited real goods, shouldn't we? However, with our busy schedules, we seem to have less time to "smell the flowers along the way." Even though we have more labor saving devices freeing us from mundane household duties(for example, dishwashing by hand), we seem slaves to another master - the tyranny of the urgent.

We confuse immediate demands with more important - but less urgent - tasks. Many times the former come from phone calls, unannounced visits, routine appointments or household duties. Some of these must be done, but are not important in the long term. As Charles Hummel states in his excellent booklet **Tyranny of the Urgent**: "We live in constant tension between the urgent and the important." **23**

The problem is one of priorities. Gordon MacDonald phrases it this way, ". . .where your priorities are, there your time will be." **24** He recommends budgeting your time just like you would your money. Hummel suggests using a daily quiet time of meditation and prayer to prioritize your tasks for that day. MacDonald uses the example of how Jesus budgeted His time. He didn't accomplish everything He could have, but completed those tasks for which He was sent(His mission). Jesus also set limits on the use of His time.

Using Our Leisure Time

Today the issue becomes how to best utilize constructive use of our leisure time. After we have done the essential - and sometimes urgent - tasks, what do we do? Do we watch television, rent a video, listen to music, read newspapers, magazines, or books, walk, jog, or bike, talk on the phone, visit with family or friends, sleep, drive around town, go out to eat and then to a movie, concert, play or sports event or travel to a scenic destination? These are just some of the possibilities. How can we prioritize these activities so we will participate in those leading to the acquisition of Aristotle's unlimited real goods?

Both Aristotle and Maslow would use the following criteria to determine which of the above activities would lead to the "good life:"

1. Which activities would involve stimulating conversations?(belonging, love)

2. Which activities would lead to an increased sense of self-esteem?(esteem)

3. Which activities would assist in reaching a person's potential?(self-actualization)

4. Which activities would lead to an increase in knowledge and understanding? (know, understand)

5. Which activities would lead to a greater appreciation of beauty?(aesthetic)

In relating the above criteria to the possible leisure activities mentioned previously, several general observations can be made. **First**, the quality of the activity is more important than its quantity. Conversing or reading about ideas is more enriching than discussing people or things(see quote in "Introduction"). Soundness of sleep is more restful than the number of hours per night. The type of exercise is more important than its duration.

Second, active pursuits are generally more enriching than passive ones. Exercising or reading are more stimulating than watching television, videos, movies, concerts or plays. Just as physical exercise keeps the body in shape, so mental exercise keeps the mind alert.

Third, some seemingly passive pursuits form the basis for creative ideas. For example, when we are driving, walking, listening to music, or showering, a solution to a problem we have been wrestling with for days may pop into our head. Since we weren't consciously thinking about this problem, from where did the solution come? Did God speak to us? Possibly. More likely, as our brain was relaxed, the intuitive or right side of the brain became dominant, producing this idea. Therefore, all daydreaming isn't a waste of time. Tell Thomas Edison's teachers that!

Fourth, some pursuits - even though passive - can appeal to the highest level(aesthetic). Watching a gorgeous sunset over the ocean, or hiking to a pristine mountain lake, could add meaning to the Psalmist's description of seeing God in Nature. **25** The overused cliche "totally awesome" would apply in these situations. If traveling to observe this type of scenery was involved, this activity would lead to the highest form of happiness(aesthetic), according to Aristotle and Maslow.

Conclusions

What have we learned in this lesson from the emigrants that can be applied to our lives today? **First,** when purchasing real goods, we should buy those which meet only our needs, realizing needs will vary with variables as family size and geographic location. **Second,** if we purchase more than is needed(apparent goods), make sure these limited real goods do not interfere with spending on the pursuit of unlimited real goods. **Third,** our days should be budgeted to leave adequate leisure time for pursuing the unlimited real goods.

My examples from the lives of the pioneers serve to compare and contrast their uses of time and money with ours. By using the ideas of Aristotle and Maslow, I provide a framework from which to pursue the "good life." However, the real application will come as you make your own decisions as to the use of your time and money in your situations. Hopefully, this lesson will raise your consciousness for these important ideas.

The emigrants have now made the decision to journey to Oregon. They have determined what supplies to take or leave at home. Now they must figure how to find the way. This is the subject of the next chapter. Stay on the trail!

Lesson Three

"Rest Stop in Oregon"

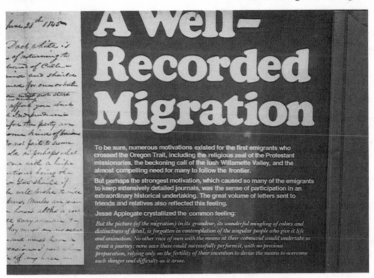

A Well-Recorded Migration

To be sure, numerous motivations existed for the first emigrants who crossed the Oregon Trail, including the religious zeal of the Protestant missionaries, the beckoning call of the lush Willamette Valley, and the almost compelling need for many to follow the frontier.

But perhaps the strongest motivation, which caused so many of the emigrants to keep extensively detailed journals, was the sense of participation in an extraordinary historical undertaking. The great volume of letters sent to friends and relatives also reflected this feeling.

Jesse Applegate crystallized the common feeling:

But the picture (of the migration) in its grandeur, its wonderful mingling of colors and distinctness of detail, is forgotten in contemplation of the singular people who give it life and animation. No other race of men with the means at their command would undertake so great a journey; none save these could successfully perform it, with no previous preparation, relying only on the fertility of their invention to devise the means to overcome each danger and difficulty as it arose.

GUIDES AND GUIDEBOOKS: FINDING THE WAY

Responsible **guides** and reliable **guidebooks** were both important to the pioneers as they started the long 2,000 mile journey to Oregon. Because they brought their democratic tradition to the frontier, selecting leaders by majority vote was the preferred method. The emigrants rejected the authoritarian claim to power a strong guide could have made. Instead a potential guide must prove himself to the wagon train families. What **characteristics** were important to their **election** as a wagon train guide? Do we look for the same characteristics in our leaders today?

Guidebooks furnished the need for information about the Trail, especially assisting the Great Migration of 1843. However, there were several versions offering conflicting advice. How did the pioneers know which books were reliable? Should they take cutoffs to save time? How high was the risk factor in these shortcuts? What can we learn about using reliable information today?

Leadership Characteristics

First the human factor - the selection of a guide. What

leadership **characteristics** did they possess? According to David Lavender, men vying for this position were by nature movers and shakers, assertive, agressive, self-reliant and ingenious at "making do." They were also undisciplined, quarrelsome and - in the frontier spirit - resentful of barriers threatening their freedom. **26** Typically, these leaders possessed both good and bad characteristics.

How do these characteristics compare to the **political** and **business leaders** we have in America today? In comparing the 1992 candidates for President of the United States, many Americans admired a "take charge" person. Witness the groundswell of support for Ross Perot, the billionaire businessmen and potential presidential candidate who pledged to "clean up" Washington. His "Rambo style" of outspokenness and decisiveness appealed to millions of his volunteers. However, his subordinates thought him too dictatorial and abrupt. His sudden departure from and re-entry into the political scene was also indicative of his unpredictability. In spite of this unpredictability, Perot still netted a respectable nineteen percent of the popular vote. He is still a powerful political force with his "United We Stand" organization. He may run again in 1996. Who knows?

Conversely, President Bush was portrayed as a "milk toast" and indecisive president who changed positions on issues. Remember his famous broken pledge: "Read my lips. No new taxes." However, his Gulf War leadership combatted this image, as his dramatic rise in the public opinion polls during and immediately after this war attested. Democratic candidate Bill Clinton's campaign was plagued with images of "slickness" and untrustworthiness. His character seemed to be more important to the electorate than his issue stands. However, he overcame these charges and focused on the economy and the issue of change. Today we call him Mr. President!

Lee Iacocca, former CEO of Chrysler Motors, was admired for his outspokenness in challenging the foreign automobile market. His reputation for innovation and making decisions contrary to his advisors evoked praise from many Americans who didn't have to work with him.

There seems to be dichotomy between what is admired in a leader from afar as opposed to a working relationship. Independence and decisiveness are considered positive traits by the former group. Consensus-building and being a team player are important to work associates. Possibly the wagon train captains were able to blend these characteristics on the Trail. The longer the journey progressed, the greater the need for cooperation by both leaders and followers.

Election of Leaders: Pioneers and Today

Selection of wagon train captains differed from our political elections in two significant methods. **First**, the election did not take place until the wagon train was about 100 miles from their starting point. This provided a trial - or "trail run" - to judge the competency of a potential leader. The potential voters - only males - could then see if this acting guide had the "right stuff."

What if a preliminary election were held nominating a Presidential candidate? The winner would be given three months to prove his competency(we already evaluate a candidate's first 100 days in office). After this trial period a final election would be held to ratify or negate the original choice. If a majority of voters disapproved this initial choice, another election would be held with different candidates until one was ratified. In our electronic age frequent elections could be held at home using the telephone and computer tabulations. Ross Perot advocates this type of direct democracy.

This selection process - without the technology - would be similar to that used by the pioneers to select their guide. By adopting the pioneer timing of elections, voters could judge candidates once in office. It'd be like voting for incumbents all the time. A restructuring our of political system would be needed for this electoral change.

Second, the selection of the wagon train guide was by **open ballot**. Lavender describes the process this way: . . . "the candidates stood in a row behind the all-male electorate. At a given signal the vote-seekers marched away across the prairie. The general mass broke after them 'lick-a-ty split,' each man forming in behind his favorite, so that every candidate flourished a sort of tail of his own, and the man with the longest tail was elected(is this where the phrase "coattails" originated?) (parentheses mine.) This was really running for office." **27**

Even though the above system differs significantly from our **secret ballot** system, there are similarities. **First,** it allows for politicking right up to the time and place of the election. That's what political campaigns are all about - "peaking" the candidate on Election Day. **Second,** the influence of public opinion and peer pressure is obvious. Even though we vote with no one around, we may consider what the latest polls and our family and friends think about the candidates before stepping into the voting booth.

You can see a similarity of characteristics between the emigrant guides and today's political candidates. However, the selection process differs significantly. The pioneers were now ready to place their trust in their guides - until they disagreed with them! Being an independent lot, they had no qualms holding another election. They had the ability to hold elections whenever needed.

This is unlike our Presidential elections occurring every four years. In the United States the President tries to manipulate events to put the most favorable "spin" on them during the campaign. The political term "October surprise" refers to the incumbents ability to "create" favorable news right before the election. A candidate cannot control the timing of elections, but instead attempts to control events.

Guidebooks: The Need For Information

For early emigrants, the need for reliable information was important. The first report was mapped by Captain John C. Fremont, the pathfinder who only journeyed to South Pass. To provide information on the western half of the Trail, the federal government printed excerpts from the report of Lieutenant Charles Wilkes' 1841 naval expedition to the Columbia River. These guides included "information about mileage references, locations for major stream and river crossings, spring sites, availability of grass, comments about the nature of the road and major sites or attractions." **28**

Aside from these official reports, conflicting information came from more personal sources. Philip Edwards, who had traveled West in 1834, wrote a letter in 1842 answering questions about Oregon. He painted a positive picture of the fertile Willamette Valley, together with its healthful climate and spectacular scenery. However, Edwards included one discouraging report - wagons could not cover more than two-thirds of the journey. The opposite view was expressed by Marcus Whitman, the missionary who had traveled West and assisted in guiding the Great Migration of 1843. He was just as emphatic that wagons could travel the entire Trail. **29** How did the pioneers resolve this dilemma? They ultimately took a risk(discussed in Lesson One) and followed Whitman's advice by taking wagons past Fort Hall to Fort Vancouver. From there they crossed the Columbia River to Oregon City and the Willamette Valley.

Why did the emigrants follow the advice of Whitman rather than Edwards? There may have been two reasons. **First**, Whitman gave the advice in person, whereas the "wagon warning" came impersonally through a letter in a newspaper. There's no substitute for personally making a convincing argument about a particular issue. **Second**, Marcus Whitman carried the moral authority of a missionary. Edwards was a private citizen. Even though both men had previously traveled the Trail, the pioneers probably perceived Whitman as more credible. These same two reasons - personal contact and moral authority - are also important today in determining what to believe about a controversial topic.

On what types of information do we rely when traveling today? There are state roadmaps, tourism brochures, atlantes, travel guides and planning services by travel agencies. Obviously the quantity of information is much greater than 150 years ago. **Megatrends** documents the change from an agricultural(during the pioneer times) to industrial(until 1956) to the present information society. We have access to so much information today that Naisbitt states: "We are drowning in information but starved for knowledge." **30** He is also expressing the need for reliable guides in all areas, including travel.

Using Criteria To Select Information

What **criteria** can be used to determine the reliability of information today? The following are possibilities:

1. Which source presents the most **objective** information?

2. Which source presents the most **thorough** information?

3. Which source is the most **respected** by relevant experts?

4. Which source provides the largest **readership**?

5. Which source has the most well-known **author(s)**?

6. Which source is distributed by the most **credible** publisher?

In order to apply the above criteria to a real-life situation, let's assume you want to purchase a guide with maps describing and illustrating the Oregon Trail. This purchase will complement the book you are presently reading while furnishing background information as you travel the Trail. Based on your own preliminary research, you have narrowed the choices to five. How do you determine which of these to purchase?

By using an analytical approach, you could construct a grid similar to the following:

Criteria(across)	1	2	3	4	5	6	Totals
Sources(down)							
A	1	5	1	2	3	5	17
B	3	4	5	5	5	2	24
C	2	3	4	3	2	1	15
D	4	1	2	1	1	3	12
E	5	2	3	4	4	4	22

Diagram 3

Down the left vertical column list the five guidebooks you are considering(A - E above) The top horizontal column is for your criteria, identified by number from 1 - 6)(see above list). You then use a forced rating system, where each source is evaluated by each criteria on a scale of 1-6, with six being the highest rating. Under this system, you cannot have a tie in the vertical columns. However, the horizontal columns can have the same numbers. By simply tabulating horizontally the ratings for each source, you can determine which source to purchase. The highest score would be what you would purchase(Source B).

As you can see, this is a logical and methodical system. This approach is only as valid as (1) the criteria you select and (2) how carefully you evaluate each source using your criteria. Your ratings should be objective and you should not have a preconceived notion as to the final outcome. If you follow these guidelines, this method can be used - not only for purchasing guidebooks - but for any type of problem solving situation(personal or career) you may encounter.

Determining Which Cutoffs To Take

The pioneers have now selected their guide and guidebooks. Farther on the trail they face new decisions. Should they stay on the main trail or chart a new course in order to save miles and time? Later expeditions were faced with more deviations than the 1843 party. However, this question still faced the early travelers.

I will describe **four cutoffs** and alternate routes. Please refer to the map in the Introduction for their locations. The early Trail was essentially the same until the halfway point at South Pass. The **Sublette Cutoff** - first used in 1844 - avoided the more common but longer route south to Fort Bridger and then back northwesterly to Fort Hall. At the "Parting of the ways"(aptly named) the risk-takers saved 46 miles across the waterless Little Colorado Desert. The pioneers' only water came from what they could carry, or if they found standing water from the infrequent rains. Haines states this was a time for the emigrants "to decide whether to gain a few miles or favor their livestock." **31** Even today this route is considered dangerous to cross without taking special precautions and using an all-terrain vehicle.

About half the wagon trains forded the **Snake River** at the Three Island Crossing near present Glenn's Ferry, Idaho. Even though this crossing was dangerous and risky, the land on the other side was better for travel. There was probably more grass on this side(it was actually greener there!). The remaining pioneers choose a safer but more desolate route by staying on the south side of the river until reaching Fort Boise - a distance of over 100 miles. The emigrants again faced the choice between change or the status quo.

All early stops included the **Whitman Mission** near present Walla Walla, Washington. This was an important stop for those needing food, blacksmithing or medical atttention. Some even stayed the winter in a normally vacant "Emigrant House." **32**   Later in the 1840s the pioneers were better supplied and passed up their need to resupply. Instead they continued on the south side of the Columbia River until The Dalles, Oregon. Once again they needed to determine if their supplies were essential to finish the journey. With only about 200 miles to completion, this decision was relatively easy.

From The Dalles the pioneers after 1845 could decide whether to build rafts and float down the sometimes dangerous Columbia or pay a toll to travel down(literally!) the **Barlow Road**. By choosing the latter route, the emigrants encountered Laurel Hill, according to Haines probably the most difficult hill of the entire journey.

Both paths afforded difficulties. The river route presented the possibility of the rafts capsizing or crashing on rapids - with the resultant loss of their possessions and possible drowning. Laurel Hill was expensive and was therefore the choice of the wealthy. This steep descent, composed of two drops of 240 and 60 feet, also presented the possibility of losing goods to wagon crashing. Since both options presented significant dangers, the decision may have been influenced more by economics than by risk.

Choosing Paths Today: Concrete and Abstract

Today we face similar choices in choosing which paths to journey - both on concrete and metaphorical levels. When planning a trip by **automobile**, we first must decide which route to take. We then need reliable information(see the above section "Using Criteria To Select Information") to make this determination. Should we travel the faster but monotonous interstate highways, built for safety but not variety? Another option is to take the more scenic but slower "blue highways." This term, from a book by the same name, refers to the highway maps where the main routes are red and the back roads blue. **Blue Highways: A Journey Into America** chronicles the 13,000 mile route of the author(William Least Heat Moon) through small towns. Do we choose the most direct route, even though they are not interstate highways(green on the maps), or stay on the longer main route? This latter question - as we have discussed - was also faced by the pioneers.

What about our journey through **life?** What's more important to us (1) hurrying through our prime earning years to accomplish our goals(primarily career and financial) and then doing what we really want upon retirement, or (2) taking time along the way to "smell the flowers" by enjoying family, friends, the quest for knowledge and aesthetic pleasures - Maslow's higher levels?

The "Yuppies" and their "climbing the corporate ladder" in search of wealth and status symbols(such as BMWs) epitomized the "Me Decade" of the 1980s. These "baby boomers" would more likely agree with the first lifestyle above. Conversely, the 1990s have seen an upsurge in persons giving up the materialistic "rat race" for the simpler and slower pace of small town and country living. Our present time period could be labeled the "We Decade."

Time magazine, which seems to make national trends official, devoted its April 8, 1991 cover story to "The Simple Life." The article summarizes the change: "In place of materialism, many Americans are embracing simpler pleasures and homier values. They've been thinking hard about what really matters in their lives, and they've decided to make some changes. What matters is having time for family and friends, rest and recreation, good deeds and spirituality." **33** This quote reflects the second lifestyle above.

Application: Which choice are you presently making?

Another decision we make on life's journey is what **belief system** we follow in our search for the "good life." We may not consciously adhere to a particular philosophy of life, but we all have one. Burton Porter's excellent book **The Good Life: Alternatives In Ethics** summarizes and critiques several basic views on life.

Their philosophies and main emphases are:

Hedonism(seeks pleasure while avoiding pain)

Self-Realization(seeks fulfillment through reaching our potential)

Naturalism(finds meaning through closeness to Nature)

Duty(attempts to perform actions that are right)

Religion(believes in God and accepts His Word as authoritative)

Existentialism(finds meaning through understanding ourself)

As the above philosophies illustrate, the "good life" can be different for each individual. You may subscribe to one or a combination of the above views, or adopt another viewpoint.

Application: Which of the above philosophies comes closest to your view of the "good life?"

Another path we can choose through life is to follow the majority view on issues or determine our own path, if different from the majority. Thus the question, "Who determines our beliefs and actions - the crowd or ourselves?" Answers to this question can be answered by the following continuum depicting locus of control:

Locus of Control

External   Internal

A person with a high external locus of control would be more susceptible to going along with the majority, even if their ideas contradict what he thinks is right. Conversely, a person exhibiting a high internal locus of control will be more apt to do what she thinks is right, even if most persons disagree with her. There may be a direct correlation between an individual's high sense of self-esteem and his high internal locus of control. Also a person with a low sense of self-esteem may possess a high external locus of control. Lesson one dealt with the relationship between self-esteem and risk-taking.

Individuals throughout history have spoken or written about choosing minority viewpoints. Jesus warns of the wide path leading to destruction and advocates the narrow path leading to salvation. **34** The Apostle Peter, when warned by the Jewish leaders not to preach about Jesus, stated emphatically: "We must obey God rather than man." **35** The poet Robert Frost closes his famous poem "The Road Not Taken" with these words:

> "Two roads diverged in a wood, and I -
> I took the one less traveled by,
> And that has made all the difference." **36**

Conclusions

What **lessons** have we learned from the pioneers? **First,** leadership characteristics need to be evaluated carefully in selecting political leaders. The pioneers did this in selecting their guides. **Second**, our type of election system(when and how often we hold them) reflects the types of leaders we choose. The emigrants held their election after the guide had shown his leadership capabilities. **Third**, we need criteria to select reliable information. The pioneers needed this in determining which guidebooks to use. **Fourth,** we need to determine our life philosophy for finding the "good life." The pioneers saw their "good life" in more concrete terms and found it in Oregon. **Fifth**, we need to resolve to do what we think is right, even if we are in the minority. Some pioneers choose the cutoffs because they thought it was the right thing to do at the time.

Reflect on these lessons as you continue your "journey." Next we focus on the most important single resource of the trip - water.

Lesson Four

WATER: LIFEBLOOD OF THE JOURNEY

Importance Of Water

Water - one of the essentials of life. Approximately three-fourths of the earth is covered with it. Our bodies comprise roughly the same water percentage as the earth. Is this coincidental or by "grand design?" Farmers and city dwellers alike complain when we receive too much rain - flooding fields and lawns. When the heavens are shut, causing a drought, these same fields and lawns burn. But we agree on one point - we need water to sustain life. This is definitely one of Maslow's basic physiological needs.

Water is also important in a figurative sense. The well known 23rd Psalm paints a relaxing picture "beside the still waters." The Psalmist also draws an analogy between the deer panting for water and David's thirst for the living God. **37** When Jesus encountered the woman at the well, he contrasted her need for the water she was drawing(she would become thirsty again) with the water He could give her - watering her forever with eternal life. **38** The classic song "Ole Man River" portrays the continuity of life as "he just keeps rolling along." Water is used throughout literature as a metaphor to relax, refresh and renew us.

Rivers were the most important determinants in locating cities in the Eastern and Midwestern United States.

By looking at an atlas, you can correlate major rivers with major metropolitan areas. Pittsburgh is on the confluence of the Ohio, Allegheny and Monongahela Rivers(football fans have heard of Three Rivers Stadium). The Mississippi(the longest river in the United States) is home to the Minnesota Twin Cities, St.Louis(also intersected by the Missouri River), Memphis and New Orleans at its mouth. The Missouri River, followed by Lewis and Clark in 1804-6, is important to Kansas City and Omaha.

The three main rivers followed by the pioneers were the Platte, Snake and Columbia. Compared to the Eastern and Midwestern rivers, the population centers along them today are much smaller, even though the population of the country is moving West(remember **Megatrends**). Interestingly, the largest metropolitan centers along the entire Trail are at the beginning(Kansas City, Missouri) and end(Portland, Oregon). The only other metropolitan areas(100,000 or greater population) are Topeka, Kansas and Boise, Idaho. Early maps characterized most of the Trail as passing through the "Great American Desert." Because of this arid country, most emigrants passed through on their way to Oregon and California instead of settling along the Trail. This trend continues today. Today's maps show most metropolitan areas in the West located along the Pacific Coast.

Why Water Was Important To The Pioneers

The pioneers also knew the importance of water. Aside from its benefits for human and animal consumption and cooking, it provided adequate moisture to grow trees and grass. Trees were important as a primary source of wood for cooking and campfires. Traveling near trees would also provide shade during the day and when camping at night. Grass was essential for the livestock. Traveling through grass also meant less dust to "eat," especially when the winds fiercely blew. So important were water, wood and grass that Bernard Reid, when encamped near South Pass, called these basics "the emigrant's trinity of good things." **39**

Traveling near rivers usually meant finding the lowest elevation and broad plains, especially along the Platte and North Platte. However, banks of the Snake and Columbia Rivers were steep at times, forcing the emigrants to choose between closer proximity to rivers over steeper terrain versus traveling a greater distance from water on a more level plain. These choices were responsible for some of the cutoffs discussed in lesson three.

Today's transportation network still follows major rivers. As you follow the Trail along the major rivers mentioned above, you will notice freight and coal trains at your side. You have undoubtedly encountered many trucks on I-80(comprising one-third of this interstate's traffic) thundering down and past you! This is the main transportation route in the United States - as it was 150 years ago.

Description Of Pioneer Rivers And Crossings

Based on my observations and Haines' **Historic Sites Along The OREGON TRAIL,** I will provide mental images of the rivers followed by the pioneers. The Oregon Trail map in my book will also be helpful. I will only describe the rivers the emigrants actually followed - not those they crossed.

After crossing the Missouri, the **Kansas or Kaw River** was followed for about 75 miles. This tree-lined river was seldom fordable and was considered dangerous to cross. Matthew Field describes his 1843 experience this way: "We crossed the Kansas[90 miles out] upon a pirogue, a species of water craft . . . as a raft constructed on two canoes . . . vehicles and their contents were floated over, where the stream was about two hundred yards wide, with a rapid, turbid and deep current, and then the animals were made to swim across. . ." **40**

Next was the small tree-lined **Little Blue,** followed for approximately 100 miles through Kansas and Nebraska. The pioneers traveled on its East side and did not have to cross it.

The wide **Platte**(from an Indian word meaning flat),

first crossed 14 miles west of Fort Kearny at mile 333, provided a level corridor for approximately 125 miles through the "Coast of Nebraska." This river was known as being "a mile wide and a foot deep" - as it is today. The banks were sandy, slowing down the wagons. Reaching this river marked the completion of the first stage of the journey. The emigrants were now entering the higher, arid country of the buffalo.

Around mile 425 the Platte divided into the North and South Platte Rivers. The South Platte was crossed at various points, but the most popular place was the **Lower California Crossing**(mile 485), used later by the "forty-niners." This ford consisted of traveling "from three-quarters to one and a half miles . . through shallow water covering a bottom of shifting sand." **41** This ford was the most picturesque and least troublesome so far.

The **North Platte** became the next lifeline for 280 miles. This river was not as wide as the Platte. The adjacent land was more barren as the pioneers' elevation gradually increased. Still the trees along the river provided the needed fuel. This river was crossed either northeast(Mile 766) or southwest(Mile 774) of present Caspar, Wyoming. Samuel Penter describes the first crossing in 1843: ". . . North Platte, we tied all the wagons together. Someone had a long rope which was tied to the ring of the first wagon and men on the other side helped the train across." **42** This crossing was the most dangerous so far.

The clear and cold **Sweetwater River** was different than the muddier and wider Platte Rivers. The former was followed for about 100 miles from Independence Rock to South Pass. According to William Ghent, the Sweetwater "was named for its beautiful clear cold waters having a sweetish taste, caused by alkali held in solution . . . not enough, however, to cause any apparent injurious effects. . ." **43** Even though this river was fairly narrow, it was crossed at many different places. Most of these crossings were difficult because the river flowed through a narrow pass with steep rock walls on one side.

The **Bear River Valley** was the first time where the scenery became more green than brown. Trees grew on mountain foothills, providing a pleasant change of aesthetic beauty. It provided the pioneers with a great deal of curiosity during this part of the journey. The **Bear River** was followed for about 35 miles, including the steepest descent so far into the valley.

At Ft. Hall, near present Pocatello, Idaho, the **Snake River** became the lifeline for 330 miles. This river was probably the most important one for the pioneers, since they followed it longer than any other. The river curves and meanders as would a giant snake through steep barren and volcanic hills. Today this river flows slow, smooth and wide. Before hydroelectric and flood control dams and crop irrigation, the Snake would have been deeper and faster - making crossings more difficult.

Three Island Crossing, near Glenn's Ferry, Idaho, was always considered difficult. Even though the river was wide at this point(John C. Fremont calculated a breath of 1,049 feet and a depth of from six to eight feet deep **44)**, the pioneers choose this spot because there were three islands. However, the crossing only touched two of them. Most emigrants crossed here to avoid the rough, dry trail on the south side. This crossing is re-enacted today every August at Three Island State Park. Even though the water is usually low in the summer, and horses instead of oxen are used, this crossing can be dangerous. One year a horse drowned!

Those who used the south alternate route crossed the Snake(one of the cutoffs discussed in Lesson Three) by Ft. Boise(Mile 1510). Irene Paden explains, "the emigrants of 1843 and John C. Fremont (had) to borrow or hire . . . enormous dugout canoes for transporting wagons across the river." **45** At Farewell Bend(Mile 1550) the emigrants saw the Snake River for the last time as it curves to the east. An Oregon state park is now at this landmark.

Once the pioneers crossed the Blue Mountains in Oregon, they found adequate fresh water by following several small but swift rivers. Both the **Burnt and Umatilla Rivers** were followed for about 40 miles. The latter river was crossed at Mile 1712 and allowed the emigrants to follow the Columbia River on the dry, south side.

The **"Great River of the West"(Columbia)** was then followed to The Dalles(Mile 1819). Here the emigrants used rafts to float their wagons down this wide, majestic river to the end of the Trail at Oregon City - 1932 miles from Independence. After 1845 the Barlow Road could be used to avoid the Columbia River gorge.

The pioneers must have been excited to catch their first glimpse of the very wide and blue Columbia! This was their last lifeblood before reaching the Willamette Valley. As they progressed west, the banks became greener and steeper, revealing huge cliffs with thundering waterfalls. Thus the famous Columbia River Gorge. This also meant certain narrow spots contained hazardous rapids that needed to be negotiated safely. This was their last challenge before reaching their "good life" in Oregon.

Springs, Falls And An Ice Slough

Cold And Hot Springs

Even though the rivers satisfied almost all the pioneers' need for water, there were other sources meeting both basic and aesthetic purposes. Springs were always refreshing and provided relaxing campgrounds. The ice slough was a novelty not completely understood.

The first respite was at **Big Springs**(Mile 76) at a junction of the Oregon Trail near the Kansas River. **Alcove Spring**(Mile 165) furnished an idyllic setting on the east bank of the Big Blue River in Kansas. Many emigrants left their mark(literally) as described by George McKinistry in 1846: ". . . is a most beautiful spring and a fall of water of 12 feet. . . . the water is of the most excellent kind . . . and is surrounded with Ash, Cotton wood & Cedar trees . . . it is an excellent place to camp for a day or two to wash, recruit the cattle. . . I this day cut the name of the spring in the rock on Table at the top of the falls . . ." **46**

The emigrants did not encounter another significant spring until they descended Windlass Hill and came upon **Ash Hollow**(Mile 505). This spring provided the best source of water for many miles along the Platte and North Platte Rivers and was a welcome resting place. **Willow Springs**(Mile 792) furnished another campground with clear, cold water, but little grass. This feature was the most noted between the crossing of the North Platte and Independence Rock.

As soon as the pioneers crossed South Pass they encountered the first water flowing westward. **Pacific Springs**(Mile 917) didn't look like a spring, but instead created a marsh appearing as a green oasis in the dry, brown landscape. This green may have helped to keep their vision of the lush Willamette Valley alive. After all, they were over halfway to their "good life." At Mile 1006 the pioneers taking the Sublette Cutoff encountered the first of two **Emigrant Springs.** Since there was little water along this route, this campground was much appreciated.

After the Bear River Valley the emigrants encountered not cold - but hot - springs in and around present **Soda Springs, Idaho**. Rufus Sage provides an overview of this area in 1842:

> "The valley of Bear river affords a number of springs strongly impregnated with various mineral properties, which cannot fail to excite the curiosity and interest of the traveler. . . .
>
> In passing their vicinity the attention of the traveler is at once arrested by the hissing noise they emit; and on approaching to ascertain the cause, he finds two circular-shaped openings in the surface . . . filled with transparent fluid in a state of incessant effervescence, caused by the action of subterranean gases.

The water of the one he finds on tasting to be excellent natural soda, and that of the other, slightly acid and beer-like. . . these . . . are known . . . as the Beer and Soda Springs, names not altogether inappropriate." **47**

Another natural curiosity was **Thousand Springs**(Mile 1363) in central Idaho. A series of streams cascaded from the north bank of the Snake River, providing the name given them by the pioneers. An **Unnamed Hot Springs**(Mile 1417) was used as a camping spot. Peter Burnett in 1843 found "its water . . . hot enough to cook an egg." **48**

Between Ft. Boise and Farewell Bend in Oregon the emigrants enjoyed the hot cluster of **Malheur Hot Springs**(Mile 1527). John C. Fremont, when passing here in 1843, calculated the temperature at 193 degrees - with the ground being too hot to walk on with bare feet. **49** The other **Emigrant Springs**(Mile 1668) was one of many good sources of water on the route over the Blue Mountains.

Two Falls

Thirty miles apart in central Idaho were two falls adding a majestic flair to the journey. **Shoshone Falls**(Mile 1337), near Twin Falls, was five miles from the main Trail. Since it plunged 212 feet into the Snake, its thundering roar could occasionally be heard by passing emigrants. This falls surpasses Niagara Falls in height; its flow has been drastically reduced in the spring and summer by field irrigation. **Upper Salmon Falls**(Mile 1366) was more than just pleasing to the eye. Since the Snake River was narrow and composed of two rapids here, it was easy for the Indians to spear the salmon ascending the river to spawn. It was here that the emigrants bartered with the Indians for this fish - a welcome meal! **50**

Ice Slough

Along the Sweetwater River before South Pass lies a

marsh in the valley. Here water collects and freezes beneath a tundra-like covering. Because of the insulating effect of this cover, the ice remained frozen during the summer. The emigrants considered this a miraculous feat of Nature. They even made Icy Sloughs - maybe a forerunner of today's slush drinks! **51** This spot also served to break the dry, monotonous journey through Wyoming.

As you can see by the above descriptions, water comes in different terrains. Its uses kept alive the people and animals along the Trail. How important is water to modern Westerners? How do we allocate this scare resource? How can we preserve this natural resource? We will focus on these issues next.

Importance Of Water Today

Water is still the most important resource in the West. Without adequate supplies the population growth experienced during the last two decades could not continue. Water is needed for crop irrigation, factory and business production, human and animal consumption, residential use and recreational enjoyment. Rural, urban and suburban residents all depend upon it. Will there be enough water for all to use - like the pioneers?

Problems Of Water Use Today

Encounters with the Future uses computer analyses of trends to predict the future. According to authors Marvin Cetron and Thomas O'Toole, "a massive shortage of water will be one of the major social and political issues of the 1990s." **52** They predict "water wars" between states experiencing the largest population growth(California, Arizona, Colorado, New Mexico, Utah and Nevada). Interestingly enough, the Oregon Trail does not intersect any of these states. The pioneers had plenty of water if they stayed close to the rivers. According to a "Water-Resource Regions" map in **Places Rated Almanac**, the six "Oregon Trail states" (Missouri, Kansas, Nebraska, Wyoming, Idaho and Oregon) have plenty of water today. **53**

Recently some Western states have experienced six consecutive years of drought. You have probably read about these "dry" states making agreements with the "wet" states for more water rights. Water from rivers such as the Colorado are sought after by all types of users. The agricultural interests, who use the vast majority of water, want to protect it from encroachment by the rapidly expanding metropolitan areas. The urban interests feel they need a greater share to serve their population base. California has used voluntary conservation methods and has resorted to mandatory measures in some cases.

Even though water is a renewable resource and can be replenished through rain and snowfall, it can be depleted too quickly. This is happening to the huge High Plains Aquifer under the states of Texas, New Mexico, Oklahoma, South Dakota, Colorado, Kansas, Nebraska and Wyoming. According to the **Places Rated Almanac**, water from wells is being pumped out eight times as fast as it can be recharged from this vast reservoir. At this rate this aquifer, the main source of water for the West, could begin to dry up around the year 2000. **54**

The draining of the rivers - especially the Platte and Snake - for crop irrigation provides less wetlands for wildlife and migratory birds such as the Sandhill Cranes in Nebraska. As a result conflicts arise between agricultural and environmental water users.

Another problem relates to the pollution levels of the rivers. Because of industrial wastes, chemical runoffs and human recreational use, the Columbia River is listed as endangered - and it's not a plant or animal! The pioneers also polluted rivers with human and animal wastes - but not to this level. What can be done to preserve these life-giving rivers and its wildlife, conserve existing water sources and increase water sources?

Solutions To Water Usage Today

In order to preserve the rivers and supporting wild-life, **political action** is needed. Both on the national and state levels, strong water pollution laws are needed to regulate the wastes resulting from business and agricultural uses. It is not enough to pass these laws. Enforcement by the appropriate executive agencies are needed, including the administration of strong penalties. Setting aside more areas for wetland use would assist in strengthening this valuable ecosystem.

As a private citizen concerned about these issues, joining such environmental interest groups as the Sierra Club, or contacting your appropriate senator or representative, would make an impact and provide you with a sense of political efficacy(the feeling that your efforts are worthwhile).

Voluntary conservation efforts will help assure adequate supplies and possibly prevent the imposition of mandatory measures. With minimal planning businesses and individuals could accomplish the following conservation acts: installing more efficient shower heads, purchasing water saving sinks and stools, flushing less, washing dishes and clothes with full loads and using recycled water for lawns and washing cars. The "less is more" philosophy - important in this age of scarce resources - would then become a lifestyle.

California, the bellweather state for change, is considering using two methods to increase its water supply. One costly approach is desalinization, the process of removing saltwater from the oceans to provide drinking water. This method has been used in the dry Middle East. A novel approach predicted in **Encounters with the Future** sees the United States "towing glaciers out of the Arctic to East and West Coast ports where they'll be tapped for their water." **55** Watch California for these new developments.

Other states have seeded the clouds with chemicals to produce more rain. This approach is costly and has mixed results. A less costly approach is to simply pray for rain. As drought conditions worsen, groups have gathered for prayer services. If they receive immediate results, their faith in an all-powerful God would be affirmed. They could then identify with job that God is indeed in control of Nature. **56** Doubters would conclude the precipitation would have come eventually.

Conclusions

What have we learned from the pioneers through our study of the importance of water? **First,** this precious resource is just as important to us today as it was to the pioneers. **Second,** our involvement in the political process is important to protect our waterways and wetlands. **Third,** our individual conservation efforts will provide more water for future users. **Fourth,** even though we can use the above efforts to preserve our existing water supplies, only Nature's God can determine when the rain will fall on the "just and the unjust." For that we should be grateful.

This lesson dealt with a natural phenomenon - water. The next lesson will discuss essential man-made structures - forts and missions. They were also oases on the journey. Keep traveling!

Lesson Five

"Ft. Hall, Pocatello, ID"

FORTS and MISSIONS: OASES ON THE PLAINS

In addition to depending upon water for their journey, the emigrants also needed forts and missions. All forts provided opportunities to purchase supplies. Some forts also provided blacksmithing services for their animals, performed wagon repairs and exchanged mail. The missions - in addition to furnishing supplies - could provide another need - spiritual. Both places provided time for rest, relaxation and restoration.

This lesson will describe seven forts and four missions important to the pioneers. Sources will be Haines' **Historic Sites Along THE OREGON TRAIL**, brochures obtained from my visits, together with my observations. Today's applications will center around the following three needs important to the pioneers:

1. The need for protection and safety from hostile humans
2. The need for spiritual guidance
3. The need for rest, relaxation and restoration

Forts

In 1844 the Secretary of War recommended establishing a chain of forts from the Missouri River to the Rockies to protect the ever increasing emigrant travel along the Oregon Trail. The goal was to construct a fort every 300 miles along the Trail. In 1848 **Fort Kearny** (Mile 320) - named for a famous general - became the first fort along the Trail. It was an open fort, with mainly sod and adobe buildings. Even though it was considered uncomfortable and unhealthy, it was busy and important - since it was the first and easternmost supply center on the Trail. **57**

Today this site is a Nebraska Historical Park eight miles southeast of Kearney. On the grounds is a replica of a stockade fort - unlike the open original - complete with four corner guard stations. The 80 acre grounds, covered with many cottonwood trees, also includes rifle pits, a grass-covered mound for munitions, and a powder storeroom. You can still see part of the original foundation and the flagmast.

This fort has special significance for me. While our family lived in the City of Kearney, I frequently visited Ft. Kearny(spelled different than the city). Through the historical knowledge of a friend (Jay Nugent, from Urbandale, Iowa), I became interested in this fort and the Oregon Trail. This fort, coupled with Nebraska's tourist slogan proclaiming "Nebraska: The Good Life," prompted the book you are reading. By combining the history of the Oregon Trail with the pioneers' search for the "good life," I hope to make their experiences meaningful for you.

Fort Laramie (originally Fort John) at Mile 650 provided for both real and apparent goods (remember Aristotle's distinction between the two?). Fort John was built by the American Fur Company in 1841 on high ground overlooking the Laramie River. It was the most important fort along the journey. John C. Fremont describes it thus: ". . . its lofty walls, whitewashed and picketed, with the large bastions at the angles, gave it quite an imposing appearance . . . the fort, which is a quadrangular structure, built of clay . . . walls are about fifteen feet high, surmounted with a wooden palisade, and form a portion of ranges of houses, which entirely surround a yard of about one hundred and thirty feet square." 58

Even though this fort was located in a barren, bleak, treeless land, it provided ". . . an island of civilization in the western wilderness. . . " 59 Timber had to be hauled from the Laramie Mountains, 100 miles distant. In addition to providing the essential supplies (real goods), wagons could be repaired and repacked and blacksmithing services were available. There was even a postal service. This was usually the first word the emigrants received from friends and relatives back East. The women could even buy civilized clothes (apparent goods) and wash their trail-worn ones. Time for dancing and relaxation was also available.

Today Fort Laramie is a National Historic Site, complete with tours and living history demonstrations. Visitors can stroll the open grounds and observe the cooks working in the bakery. To illustrate the importance of fresh food, an armed guard was once stationed to protect a single tomato plant! I don't know if it was ever eaten. The tour takes you through some of the restored buildings, including officers' quarters, barracks, the livery and jail. There is even a demonstration of how men breaking strict rules were disciplined - chained to a cannon ball in a stooping position in the hot sun!

After crossing South Pass, and staying on the main route, the emigrants reached **Fort Bridger** at Mile 1025 and 6,700 feet elevation. This structure was a trading post built around 1844 and operated by the legendary mountain man Jim Bridger. Heinrich Lienhard and William Clayton described the fort as consisting of two blockhouses, four log houses and a small enclosure for horses surrounded by ten foot high palisades. Lienhard concluded this fort "could hardly be defended for long against a determined attack." 60 Even though this post was not as elaborate at Fort Laramie, it provided for essential supplies and repair work. You could even trade your worn-out animals for newer models. Sounds like today's automobile deals!

After heading northwesterly again for approximately 200 miles, the pioneers came to the place where they were supposed to leave their wagons - **Fort Hall**. This advice was followed by the wagon trains in 1841 and 1842. The Great Migration of 1843 - persuaded by Marcus Whitman - broke this precedent and rolled all the way to Oregon. This accomplishment was the single most important factor in securing the Oregon Country for the United States in its land dispute with Great Britain.

This trading post, erected by Nathaniel Wyeth in 1843, was a stockade 80 feet square. It was another important stop for sup plying the real goods. However, John Boardman in 1843 described it this way: ". . . Fort Hall is situated in a large plain on the Snake River & built of Squaw cakes of mud baked in the sun; it is inferior to Fort Laramie . . . there was neither meat, flour nor rice to be had. Nothing but sugar and coffee at 50 cents per pint." **61**

Today the original fort is located on the Fort Hall Indian Reservation, where access is difficult. However, a replica of the original fort is located in Ross Park in Pocatello, Idaho. After failing to find the original fort, I visited this replica - complete with its white walls.

The emigrants traveled another 300 miles through Idaho to find **Fort Boise.** A trading post of the famous Hudson's Bay Company (HBC), it was built in 1834. Similar to Fort Hall, it was also located on the east bank of the Snake River and was made of wood encased with adobe. John C. Fremont describes this post as "a simple dwelling-house" (with the) . . . post being principally supported by salmon." **62** The pioneers were able to buy real goods - no apparent goods here.

The original fort was severely damaged by flood waters in 1853 and may not have been used after that. In driving on a rutted dirt road in search of the original fort, I did find a unique monument marking this spot. This concrete structure combined symbols depicting the British influence, white-Indian confrontations, topped with a lion's head. A replica of this fort can be seen today in Old Fort Boise Park in Parma, Idaho. It is similar in appearance to Fort Hall.

220 miles later the early emigrants stopped at **Fort Walla Walla**, on the east bank of the "Great River of the West." This was another HBC trading post that provided company boats to transport essential supplies and passengers down the dangerous Columbia. This post also furnished the opportunity to trade in weary livestock for fresh ones, upon their arrival in the Willamette Valley. Irene Padden describes the fort this way: "It was about two hundred feet square, and was built tightly of timbers set on end. At opposite corners, square bastions, supported on sturdy legs, projected out beyond the enclosure. . . " **63** This fort looked rugged with its timbered appearance - the way we usually visualize forts today.

The last oasis on the emigrants' long journey was **Fort Vancouver** (Mile 1900) - headquarters of the HBC on the Columbia River. This trading post - established in 1824 - was the largest in the West in the 1840s. Its fifteen foot high Douglas-fir posts comprised the stockade enclosing an area of 734 by 318 feet - roughly one by two and one-half football fields in size. Today you can see this reconstructed fort and five major buildings (blacksmith's shop, bakery, kitchen, Indian trade shop and dispensary, wash house and the Chief Factor's residence).

The generosity of chief factor John McLoughlin encouraged the emigrants to settle in Oregon. John Boardman describes McLoughlin's kindness in 1843: "Fort Vancouver . . . well received by Doct. McLoughlin, who charged nothing for the use of his boat sent up for us, nor for the provisions, but not satisfied with that sent us plenty of salmon and potatoes, furnished us house room, and wood free of charge, and was very anxious that all should get through safe." **64**

The early 1840s saw the United States and Great Britain negotiating for the land of the Oregon Country, which now includes the states of Idaho, Oregon, Washington and the portions of Montana and Wyoming west of the Continental Divide. Ironically, McLoughlin's assistance was a factor in dividing the Oregon Country between the two countries at the 49th parallel. This meant Fort Vancouver became part of the United States in 1846.

Missions

Contrary to the chain of forts interspersed somewhat evenly along the Trail, two missions were at the beginning and two at the end of the journey. Possibly the first campground used by the emigrants was at **Shawnee Mission** (Mile 15). This mission was operated by the Methodists for educating the Shawnee Indian children. Haines claims this mission "marked the limit of civilization," since it was in Indian Territory. **65**

Approximately 100 miles later the pioneers could stop at **St. Mary's Mission,** located on the east bank of the Kansas River. This site was near the present town bearing the same name. This was a Catholic mission established among the Potawatomie Indians in 1848. These Indians "were helpful to the emigrants as ferrymen and provisioners." **66** These missionaries thus saw the fruits of their labors in the good deeds of their "converts."

By far the most famous religious outpost was the **Whitman Mission** (Mile 1710) - approximately 200 miles from the emigrants' destination. This mission was particularly important to the Great Migration, since Marcus Whitman served as their guide and physician. He brought the pioneers to his mission, sharing its meager food, blacksmithing and medical services. Since the main route bypassed this mission after 1844, only emigrants sick and destitute stopped for shelter and comfort.

Whitman and his wife Narcissa played important roles in the educational and spiritual development among

the Native Americans in the Oregon Country. Indians alleg-
edly visited St. Louis seeking teachers and the white man's
"Book of Heaven" - the Bible. In response the American
Board of Foreign Missions sent Rev. Samuel Parker and Dr.
Whitman to select mission sites. While Parker continued west
Whitman returned east to recruit more workers, convinced
the "fields were white unto harvest" with Indians. In 1836
Whitman returned west with his wife, Rev. Henry Spaulding
and his wife and William Gray. This journey marked the first
time white women crossed the continent by land - a signifi-
cant historical feat.

The Whitmans and Spauldings learned the Indian
languages and printed books for them - the first books pub-
lished in the Pacific Northwest. However, the Indians - being nomadic and restless - were indifferent to spiritual matters, books and school. The Whitman's - convinced of their
"calling" - continued to work with the Indians. Sunday was
observed as a day of worship and rest. They taught the Ten
Commandments and required the memorization of eleven
Bible verses per week.

After eleven years of working with the Indians, a series of misunderstandings caused a tragedy. Cultural differences between the white and Indian ways of life caused tensions. Increasing numbers of emigrants, together with stories of settlers taking Indian lands elsewhere, convinced the
Indians their way of life was in danger.

An 1847 measles epidemic brought by the whites
decimated half the Cayuse Indians - since they had no resis-
tance to this dreaded disease. Even though Dr. Whitman
treated both whites and Indians, the latter died. Convinced
of a conspiracy to eliminate their tribe, the Cayuse attacked
the mission, killing the Whitmans and fourteen others. These
killings ended the Protestant missions in Oregon and resulted
in a war against the Cayuse. The Whitmans thus became
martyrs and this tragedy was instrumental in Congress creating the Oregon Territory in 1848 - the first west of the
Rockies.

Today visitors can see the mission site, together with the "Emigrant House" site, a restored millpond and the blacksmith site. The grounds are peaceful with only the noise of the gentle wind blowing through the cottonwood trees. By ascending a steep hill you can see the "Great Grave" and the Whitman Memorial. The summit affords a panorama of the green and gold farming countryside west of Walla Walla, Washington.

The **Dalles Mission** - located on the Columbia River about 100 miles from the end - "appears (according to Haines) to have rendered a greater service than Whitman's." The former mission was established in 1838 by the Methodists. The Great Migration found two dwellings, a school, stable, barn, garden and fields for the weary emigrants. **67** This was their last chance to stock up before rafting down the Columbia or traversing the Barlow Road after 1845.

Through these descriptions of forts and missions, you can see their importance to the emigrants' basic needs. Missions afforded the opportunity to address spiritual concerns. Both forts and mission afforded oases for rest, relaxation, and restoration. How important are these needs to us today? These applications will be explored next.

Need For Protection Today

Today Americans don't seek protection from forts and missions. However, we want our cities, suburbs, towns and farms to be secure. If we believe "our home is our castle," do we need a moat for protection? How safe are we in our daily environs?

Crime is a consideration for contemporary Americans, regardless of where we live. Even though the largest metropolitan areas have the highest crime rates, smaller urban and rural areas are not immune to these problems. Big city crime is also spilling into the suburbs. According to the **1990 FBI Uniform Crime Reports**, the following types of crimes increased during the 1980s by the following percentages:

+34	Violent crimes (murder, forcible rape, robbery and aggravated assault)
+5	Property crimes (burglary, larceny-theft and motor vehicle theft)
+8	Crime index total **68**

Other reports have shown approximately one of every three Americans a crime victim at sometime during their life.

Because of the increase in crime, many homes now have security systems, complete with automatic lights, bells, whistles and an alarm linked to the police headquarters. Are these systems the modern day moats for our homes? Families keep doors dead-bolt locked even when home. Windows are closed even though outside ventilation could enhance the interior environment. These measures are common sense precautions when away from home - but when home? Does this cause us to enjoy our "castles?" The degree to which we implement these measures relates to the degree of risk (openness in this case) we are willing to take. Remember this discussion in lesson one. How do we balance risk with security? Can we ever be totally secure in this world?

Several references in the Old Testament speak figuratively of forts as protection. The prophet Samuel compares Jehovah to His fortress and my Savior. **69** The Psalmist sees "The Lord as my fort where I can enter and be safe . . . my tower of strength and safety." **70** These writers see our security in God and not in man-made high-tech systems.

The Need to Address Spiritual Concerns

Missions were founded to educate and "Christianize" the Indians. The emigrants could benefit from this religious emphasis if they chose. How important is religion in American today? I will present evidence illustrating both its importance and lack of importance. You may then draw your own conclusions.

Several surveys conclude the importance Americans place on religious values. According to one poll faith in God is the most important part of Americans' lives. 40% of respondents said they valued their relationship to God above all else, while only 2% said a job that pays well was the most important thing in their life. Another poll reveals approximately one-third of Americans have a personal relationship with God. The phrase "born-again Christian" - asking Jesus Christ to take control your life - may describe these evangelicals.

In the Gallup Organization's 1990 survey of religion in America, the following questions and results were:

"How **important** would you say religion is in your life:"

Very important	58%
Fairly important	29%
Not very important	13%

"About how often do you **pray**?"

Once a day or more	52%	
Several times a week	14%	
Once a week	9%	
Less than once a week/never	25%	**71**

On the other side James Wall, editor of the **Christian Century**, sees our society as more secular than religious. Wall states his thesis in an interview for the **Christian Science Monitor**: "We give absolute freedom to the secular world view to shape society. It is the dominant religion of the culture, while the religious perspective is leashed." **72** He sees materialism - the dominant theme of the 1980s - as a by-product of our secular society. The primary value is measured in monetary success. As a result a philosophical or religious question such as "Does life have any deeper purpose to it?"(other than making money), is not seriously addressed. The conflict between the sacred and secular continues today.

The Need For Rest, Relaxation And Restoration

Forts and missions offered emigrants the opportunity to "smell the flowers" - thereby providing a welcome break in the monotonous journey. How do we slow down and "recharge our batteries" today? Is this what the weekends are made for?

The need for rest, relaxation and restoration is necessary today for three reasons. **First**, Americans are actually working more hours per week during the 1990s than in recent decades. This may be because economic conditions have produced more service sector and low-paying jobs, causing a wage earner to work more hours to maintain the same income and standard of living. Many more businesses and stores are open seven days per week, creating a demand for more workers. **Second**, more mothers are working outside the home in the job market. Today - for the first time in our nation's history - women comprise a majority of the labor force. **Third**, during our non-employed hours we try to crowd in many activities - usually on the weekends. This frenzied pursuit of leisure may be more stressful than our regular employment.

One of the most debatable issues on the Oregon Trail journey was whether to rest on Sunday. This decision was made by each wagon train. Practical as well as religious considerations were involved. Rest was needed, especially for the animals. The Genesis account of God creating the world in six days and resting on the seventh day, together with the commandment to remember the Sabbath Day as a holy day, provided further justification for stopping and holding church services. Reasons for not resting centered around the need to continue, so as to not get caught in late autumn snowstorms in the Blue Mountains.

How did we formerly spend Sundays? During the 1950s some states had "Blue Laws" requiring most stores to be closed on Sundays. During the energy crisis of the 1970s, some stores closed on Sundays - or one day per week - for conservation reasons. Society's observance of Sunday used to be governed by the Judeo-Christian ethic of worship and rest. Families seemed to have more time to enjoy cultural and recreational outings, such as going to the park for picnics or swimming in the lake.

How do we spend Sundays today? More people see this day as just another day of the week - a good time for shopping and yard work - rather than attending church. According to The Gallup Organization 40% of Americans said they attended a religious service in the last seven days. [73] Families still try to participate in cultural or recreational outings. However, this is becoming more difficult with more working mothers, fathers working more hours and children involved in more organized activities.

As you can see our society is still divided on how to spend Sunday - as were the pioneers. It seems secular pursuits have taken over the original intention expressed in the Bible and observed by earlier generations of Americans.

MacDonald's **Ordering Your Private World** relates rest and restoration, and sees them as necessary if we are to grow in maturity. Rest is not sleeping but ceasing our normal weekly routines. MacDonald sees three aspects to this Sabbath rest. **First**, it is a time for reflection, for looking back over the week to ask the following questions:

"What does my work mean?
For whom did I do this work?
How well was this work done?
Why did I do this (work?)
What results did I expect?
What (results) did I receive?" [74]

Second, we should pause to compare our priorities. We do this by "measuring our thoughts and values against the eternal truths that have been revealed through the Scripture and the mighty acts of God." [75] Attending worship services would be one way to focus on something not temporal. **Third**, we focus on the future by redefining our mission and purpose in life, and how we can fulfill it during the coming week. Remember the discussion of our mission in life in lesson one.

Conclusions

What have we learned about the pioneers' need for forts and missions that is applicable to us today? **First**, we need to feel safe in our homes like the pioneers did in the forts and missions. **Second**, we need to address our spiritual as well as temporary needs. **Third**, we need time for worship, relaxation and rest once a week, as did most of the emigrants.

Various natural landmarks served the emigrants' aesthetic needs along the journey. These features will be our next focus. Come along!

Lesson Six

"Chimney Rock, Bayard, NE"

·LANDMARKS: ENJOYING THE AESTHETIC BEAUTY

So far on our journey we have focused on Maslow's lower needs. Lesson Two discussed the importance of selecting and taking only the essential **supplies** - what Aristotle calls real goods. The need for **water** from rivers and springs was delineated in Lesson Four. Our previous lesson illustrated the need for **protection** through forts and missions.

This lesson switches to Maslow's highest level - the **aesthetic**. Landmarks along the way were important to the emigrants. **First**, they served to break the mostly monotonous journey by providing a literal "change of scenery." **Second**, specific natural phenomena also provided a signpost measuring their progress. **Third**, these unusual formations served as a source of inspiration to continue their arduous journey. **Fourth**, some landmarks were considered "totally awesome" by the passing pioneers.

This lesson will identify the following topographical features encountered along the Oregon Trail: **lone trees, bluffs, unique rock formations, hills** and a **mound, moun-**

tain peaks and ranges and a natural bridge. Even though most of these landmarks were left in their natural state by the emigrants, some attached their human print to certain rocks. Later I will address this "signing of the rocks" graffiti. Haines' description in his **Historic Sites Along THE OREGON TRAIL** will again be utilized. In addition to these descriptions, I will hypothesize their symbolic importance to the pioneers and us today. We will examine the following questions: How important are landmarks on our "journey?" How important is aesthetic beauty to us? What inspires us today? In our modern technological age, is anything "totally awesome?"

Lone Trees

There were four individual trees - each a different species - that served as landmarks along the "Great American Desert." This vast expanse covered the area from approximately the 100th Meridian to the Rocky Mountains. West of Cozad, Nebraska, is a sign marking the eastern border of this arid region. After traveling many miles across this barren plain, your eye would naturally be attracted to these reminders of the forests the emigrants left behind.

The first tree landmark was at **Lone Elm Campground**, 32 miles from Independence. Previously it was known as "Sapling Grove," "Round Grove" and "Elm Grove." William J. Ghent describes what happened to change the name ". . . Elm Grove. . . Wislizenus, in 1839, said that there then remained but, 'a venerable elm tree that must have been seen many ages'; and this, with another which he must have overlooked, was cut down for fuel by the emigrants in 1843." **76**

A different fate befell a giant cottonwood tree at **Lone Tree Station** at Mile 275 south of Hastings, Nebraska. This landmark, visible for miles on the prairie, was blown down in a windstorm in 1865. **77**

Notice how man-made features(a campground and a station) were named after these natural landmarks. I know of at least two towns today named after trees(Lone Tree, Iowa, and Lone Pine, California). Notice on your travels how many cities and towns are named after prominent geographical features. You may want to jot them down in the margins of your book.

Close to Ash Hollow(Mile 505) was another **Lone Tree**, probably the same species as those in this lowland. According to Irene Padden this tree . . . " was the only specimen for two hundred miles." This tree was probably used for firewood by the emigrants. **78**

The last significant tree landmark was in Oregon close to Flagstaff Hill at Mile 1603. This **"Lone Pine"** was particularly important to the Great Migration. However, it met the common fate of short-sighted pioneers who again reduced it to firewood. Peter Burnett, a member of this 1843 historic trek, expressed his outrage at this tree's cutting by reflecting: "This noble tree stood in the center of a most lovely valley about 10 miles from any other timber. It could be seen at a distance of many miles. . . the tree was gone. . . had fallen at last by the vandal hands. . . Some of our inconsiderate people had cut it down for fuel." **79**

Thus three of these four landmarks fell to the pioneers' axe. What does this say about having a short or a long-term outlook? The pioneers demonstrated Maslow's Hierarchy of Needs by satisfying the lower levels(firewood for fuel) before they could enjoy the aesthetic beauty of these trees. If they had had enough firewood, they would have left the trees for others to enjoy. They emphasized the short-term lower needs instead of deferring to the long-term aesthetic pleasures.

Are we like the pioneers when it comes to cutting versus preserving trees? This dilemma is played out today in the ancient forests of the Pacific Northwest. The logging industry wants to clear cut(felling all trees in a certain area), thereby fueling the construction industry and providing jobs. On the other side the environmentalists want to preserve these oldest of living things for future generations to enjoy.

Some of these trees also have curative powers for cancer. A northern spotted owl sitting in these trees further complicates this situation. President Clinton and his Secretary of the Interior Bruce Babbitt proposed a compromise that may reconcile these conflicting claims.

How can we balance the immediate with the deferred uses of our natural resources? A formula is suggested by Stephen Covey in **The Seven Habits of Highly Effective People**. He uses Aesop's fable of the goose and the golden egg as an illustration of what type of farmer **not** to be. When the greedy farmer - wanting all the precious eggs at once instead of daily - killed the goose, he ended up with no more eggs and a dead bird on his hands! In this story the goose represents production capability(PC) and the egg represents production(P). Covey's definition of effectiveness is balancing P and PC - what he calls the P/PC Balance.

Covey relates this fable to our lives by explaining: "If you adopt a pattern of life that focuses on golden eggs(P) and neglects the goose(PC), you will soon be without the asset that produces golden eggs. On the other hand, if you only take care of the goose with no aim toward the golden eggs, you soon won't have the wherewithal to feed yourself or the goose." **80**

In applying Covey's effectiveness formula to the pioneers, we can see they skewed the formula to the production(P) side by cutting down trees. They didn't replant these trees, which would have restored their production capability(PC). This same environmental imbalance is happening in the rain forests, with little thought given to reforestation. Even though the trees clearcut in the Pacific Northwest are replenished, the question is how soon new growth will replace the bare area. Thus a balance is needed between PC and P - between the short and long run uses of wood. The pioneers could have learned from "Covey's balance" in their use of trees.

Aside from practical uses, how else are trees important symbolically to us today? Their green color - whether deciduous or evergreen - is a sign of life. We associate trees with being tall, straight and strong - characteristics we seem to admire in others. If you've ever seen the giant redwoods and sequoias in California, you can attest to these attributes. You are dwarfed by their immensity. Some of the redwoods grow over 400 feet tall and seem to reach to the heavens! There is a giant sequoia(General Sherman) that is so big in circumference you can drive an automobile through it!

The Psalmist sees the godly as flourish(ing) "like palm trees, and grow(ing) tall as the cedars of Lebanon." **81** Their aesthetic value is beautifully expressed in the famous poem "Trees" by Joyce Kilmer:

> "I think that I shall never see
> A poem lovely as a tree.
>
> A tree whose hungry mouth is prest
> Against the earth's sweet flowing breast;
>
> A tree that looks at God all day,
> And lifts her leafy arms to pray;
>
> A tree that may in Summer wear
> A nest of robins in her hair;
>
> Upon whose bosom snow has lain;
> Who intimately lives with rain.
>
> Poems are made by fools like me,
> But only God can make a tree." **82**

Bluffs

The emigrants encountered two bluffs during the first one-third of their journey. As they gradually gained elevation to 3,000 feet, they saw **O'Fallon's Bluff** at Mile 445. This bluff is a low sandstone ridge and is the first of several famous landmarks along the south bank of the Platte River. Because the river was so near this bluff, only a narrow trail could be used. Consequently, you can still see wheel ruts at the Sutherland, Nebraska rest area on Interstate 80. South of these ruts today is a power plant built in a field with grazing cows. This scene provides an interesting juxtaposition of the present with the past.

The other important bluff was **Scottsbluff** at Mile 600 in western Nebraska. This massive light brown and pink sandstone feature rises 700 feet to an elevation of 4,700 feet. Approaching wagons could see this landmark for many miles as they crossed Mitchell Pass. After hiking two miles to the top, I was rewarded by seeing pine trees and a beautiful view of Laramie Peak - 100 miles distant. This landmark gives you the feel of the approaching mountains.

The name originates from Hiram Scott, who became sick and was carried by his comrades down the river. Finally, they abandoned Hiram, who was then left to die at this bluff. In this case the "law of the jungle" - survival of the fittest - applied. Such can be pioneer life - or death.

Scottsbluff was a stoic reminder of the first variety of scenery through the plains. It rekindled enthusiasm and provided optimism for the remainder of the journey. The adage, "Variety is the spice of life" applies to the pioneers' journey, as well as our own.

Bluffs rise steeply with their flat or rounded front. They can be either brown and barren or green and tree-covered. We usually think of bluffs along rivers but they can be in the arid climate along the Oregon Trail. They are usually visible for many miles and thus serve as another type of landmark.

Metaphorically, bluffs can characterize the type of life we are leading. Is it "brown and barren" with little sense of accomplishment, or "green and fertile" with satisfying experiences? Has your career, family or level of personal achievements risen steeply, only to plateau in later years?

Rabbi Harold Kushner, in **When Everything You**

Always Wanted Isn't Enough, focuses on the issue of accomplishments and death. He states: "I am convinced that it is not the fear of death, our lives ending[especially if you have the assurance of eternal life in heaven], that haunts our sleep so much as the fear that our lives will not have mattered, that as far as the world is concerned, we might as well never have lived." **83** People are afraid to die without leaving their legacy.

In order to find meaning in life, Kushner uses a Jewish teaching as a guide. The **Talmud** says everyone should do the following three things during their life:

1. Have a child
2. Plant a tree
3. Write a book **84**

Everyone of the above will outlive you and serve as a memory of your accomplishments. Writing this book completes this list for myself. How many of these three have you accomplished? As you pass these two bluffs, you may want to reflect on these questions as they apply to your life's story.

Unique Rock Formations

Through Nebraska and Wyoming several interesting rock outcroppings appeared by the Trail. A series of three appeared in western Nebraska. Later another trio was observed in central Wyoming. All six formations were given descriptive names and noted in many diaries.

The names given to the three formations in Nebraska were reminiscent of familiar shapes they left back home. Looming south of the Trail at Mile 560 were **Courthouse Rock** and the smaller **Jail Rock**, rising 400 feet from their 4,200 feet elevation. The names given showed the importance the pioneers placed on local government and justice.

Rufus Sage describes Courthouse Rock in 1841 this way: "It rises in an abrupt quadrilangular form, to a height of three or four hundred feet, and covers an area of two hundred yards in length by one hundred and fifty broad. Occupying a perfectly level site in an open prairie, it stands as the proud place of Solitude, amid here boundless domains." **85** I've seen this rock several times and it seems to change formation and color from different perspectives. I even climbed to the top in the hot Nebraska sun, surrounded by the cloudless, blue sky. You do feel the solitude that Rufus Sage mentions. It's very quiet and peaceful at the top. Only the quiet breeze and whistling train in the background attracts your attention.

Fifteen miles westward you encounter the landmark receiving more diary space than any other - **Chimney Rock**. This sandstone spire looks like an inverted funnel rising 300 feet above the plains. Captain Booneville describes his 1832 encounter with it: ". . . at this place was a singular phenomenon, which is among the curiosities of the country. It is called the Chimney. The lower part is a conical mound rising out of the naked plain; from the summit shoots up a shaft of column, about one hundred and twenty feet in height, from which it derives its name. The height of the whole . . . is a hundred and seventy five yards . . . and may be seen at the distance of upwards of thirty miles." **86** This landmark served two aesthetic purposes: it (1) broke the monotony of traveling across the "Great American Desert" and (2) signaled that the second phase of the journey through mountainous territory was ready to begin.

Even though Chimney Rock has been eroded through the years, it is still an impressive landmark today. After stopping at the new interpretive center south from Highway 92, you can drive on gravel roads to a small pioneer cemetery. From there you can hike through a brushy gully on a narrow one-half mile path to the base. The signs at the interpretive center warning of rattlesnakes were true. I only saw one cross my path. Needless to say, I went the other way and didn't bother it! At the base you can see inscriptions carved in the soft rock by the camping emigrants. This is the first rock where names were recorded for posterity. I will describe other places later and speculate on their significance.

If you want to relive the Oregon Trail experience, you can take a wagon train trek of one, three, four, or six days through Oregon Trail Wagon Train, a privately run business in Bayard, Nebraska. You can camp overnight on the prairie, sample the pioneer food during their cookouts, and listen to stories and sing around the campfire while observing the night lighting on Chimney Rock. Even though I didn't participate in these overnight excursions, I attended one of their evening cookouts, complete with pioneer stew with all the fixins. The servers were in authentic pioneer dress. After eating we rode in a bumpy covered wagon and enjoyed the campfire described above. It at least gave me a taste - literally - of pioneer life.

The shapes of the three landmarks in Wyoming varied considerably. **Independence Rock**, at Mile 815 and 5,800 feet elevation, looked like a giant turtle from a distance. Thus the descriptive name "tortoise on the prairie." Its patriotic name originated with a group of Americans who traveled to Oregon before the Great Migration and camped here on July 4. This "turtle" - the most famous landmark west of Fort Laramie - was 1,900 feet long, 700 feet wide and 128 feet high. **87**

According to research by Martin and Martin, Independence Rock was the most common place to be on the Fourth of July. This was for two reasons: (1) this point should be reached around July 4 if the pioneers hoped to reach Oregon before the winter snows and (2) it was appropriate to celebrate our nation's founding at this spot. A typical pioneer Independence Day observance included reflecting upon the significance of this day, remembering the soldiers who had given their lives to make this day possible and celebrating their freedom and liberty as Americans. They also "drank, ate, played, relaxed, made speeches, fired their guns. They cherished the memory of family and friends and the good times they left behind." As Edwin Bryant in 1846 observed "the 'glorious fourth' was celebrated here in this remote desert with more spirit and zest, than it usually is in the crowded cities of the States." **88**

Independence Rock was another place where emigrants left their "mark." Rufus Sage in 1842 expressed his contempt for this practice:

> "The surface is covered with names of travellers, traders, trappers, and emigrants, engraved upon it in almost every practicable part, for the distance of many feet above its base - but most prominent among them all is the word, 'Independence,' inscribed by the patriotic band who first christened this lonely monument of nature in honor of Liberty's birthday. I went to the rock for the purpose of recording my name with the swollen catalogue of others traced upon its sides; but, having glanced over the strange medley, I became disgusted, and, turning away, resolved, '*If there remains no other mode of immortalizing myself,* I will be content to descend to the grave *unhonored and unsung!*'" **89**

Even though I didn't leave my "mark", I climbed up Independence Rock and noticed the many who did. Some names were bigger and carved deeper than others. Does this say something about the confidence and importance these individuals placed upon themselves? Of course the contemporary "pioneers" had to leave their legacy by carving their names and initials. We still carry this tradition today.

Five miles west of Independence Rock the emigrants encountered **Devil's Gate** at 6,000 feet elevation. Fortunately the Trail did not go through this narrow precipice. Neither did I. This eerie feature was a

> "narrow cleft - 370 feet deep, 1,500 feet long and as narrow as 50 feet in some places - by which the Sweetwater River breaks through a ridge called the Sweetwater Rocks. It was a gloomy place, and violent also when the water was high, so that a satanic denomination seemed fitting." **90**

Just the sight of this landmark must have evoked sinister feelings among the pioneers. One diary thought Devil's Gate was the most interesting feature so far.

Another similar feature just west of Devil's Gate was **Split Rock**, with a base of 6,200 feet elevation. Even though it was farther from the Trail than Devil's Gate, the notch in this mountainous terrain was clearly visible. It served as a guide for several days, similar to looking through a gun sight to make sure you are "on target."

Symbolically, what do these formations mean to the emigrants and us today? **First**, each was a unique creation, with different dimensions and features. Isn't this the way we are created? Wouldn't it be a boring society if we all looked and acted the same, like robots? Maybe this uniqueness enhanced the aesthetic beauty for the pioneers and continues to do so for travelers today. **Second**, each was given a descriptive name, reminding the pioneers of something familiar in their past. In a new setting, this gives a feeling of security and is also important to Americans in our contemporary mobile society.

"Signing Of The Rocks"

In addition to Chimney and Independence Rocks, other landmarks were important - not because of their unique formations - but because of the "human element." Pioneers chose several places along the way to carve their names. Two additional places evidence these markings today - one each in Wyoming and Idaho.

Eight miles west of Fort Laramie was a mile long cliff of soft sandstone used as a convenient place for inscribing pioneer names. Hence the name **Register Cliff**. It was close to the Trail and easy for people to leave their mark. Since we still like to carve our names, a protective fence protects the remaining originals from today's vandals. This area contains the largest number of pioneer names.

Eastern Idaho contains an excellent example of more

emigrant names. **Register Rock** is a half-buried boulder 25 feet in diameter, enclosed today by a chain-link fence. The sign I saw next to these legible names states: "Register Rock / While cooking fires smoked, and livestock / watered and grazed, the early pioneer / took time to etch his passing on this and / other rocks in the area." **91**

What can we make of these pioneer carvings then and of those today? Obviously, this practice didn't start and end with these travelers. Leaving your "mark" is as old as the cave-dwellers. Maybe this is another method of "outliving yourself" - trying to identify with something that will be here when we aren't(remember the **Talmud**'s three legacies discussed earlier in this chapter).

Interestingly, the names are carved - sometimes with the date. But no other descriptions are made. So we don't know from these accounts about the accomplishments or character of the carvers. Maybe the name is enough in providing a sense of meaning for future generations. The desire to live on is apparent by these "namedroppers" of yesterday and today.

Hills and a Mound

Hills and mounds are similar features in that they rise gradually and are lower in elevation than mountains. They can be barren or covered with trees, depending on the aridity of the climate. They are usually rounded on the sides and at the top. I will describe one mound and four hills that served as landmarks to the pioneers.

Blue Mound at Mile 54 in Kansas furnished the first view for the emigrants, most of whom were "flatlanders." This landmark, visible for many miles, was "an oval tree-shaped summit with an elevation of 1,052 feet, of which 150 feet stands cleanly above the surrounding territory. This great bump on the plains(one mile long) was a favorite spot for skylarking emigrants, and many of them climbed to the top for the big view." **92**

Two hills in Nebraska and two in Oregon were significant landmarks. Traveling across Nebraska the pioneers gradually gained in elevation from approximately 1,000 to 4,000 feet. Most of the journey was gradual and they may not have realized the ascent. However, near Brule they climbed 240 feet in 1.7 miles to reach the plateau between the South and North Platte Rivers. The strain is evident today, since you can still see these ruts up **California Hill.** Many gold prospectors later used this crossing.

Fifteen miles later **Windlass Hill**(Mile 500) provided the steepest descent so far on the journey. The wagons had to navigate a 25 degree slope for about 300 feet. This figures to a vertical drop of 150 feet. Compare this to steep grades of 6% or 7% on today's modern highways. The pioneers couldn't use runaway wagon ramps like today's trucks can!

The pioneers negotiated this hill by using ropes to let the wagons and livestock gradually down. Legend speaks of using a windlass - a winch-like device with a connected rope - for mechanically lowering these wagons. However, no such device existed during this time period. The hill's name is a misnomer.

Today there is a path leading to the top of Windlass Hill. The top furnishes a panorama, complete with wagon ruts. The bottom of the hill has badly eroded from the many wagons lurching along this route. This was the steepest grade encountered at this juncture of the journey.

Toward the end of the Trail in Oregon two hills held special significance. After traveling through the barren, dusty and hot desert, the emigrants climbed **Flagstaff Hill,** near present Baker City. This spot divided the brown arid land they were leaving(Virtue Flat) from the lush valley and the tree-covered Blue Mountains they were to encounter. This was the first evidence of the green fertile lands they were seeking. This landmark boosted their tired spirits and brought their dreams closer to reality. However, they also realized these distant mountains had to be crossed before the late autumn snows started.

Today the new National Historic Oregon Trail Interpretive Center sits atop Flagstaff Hill. This "state-of-the-art" living history museum recreates pioneer life through audio and video displays based on actual diaries. There are wagon train encampments allowing you to experience pioneer life first-hand. You can also walk on interpretive trails to savor the view the pioneers first saw. The vivid wagon ruts make this visit realistic and worthwhile. I would recommend spending a half day - as I did.

For those emigrants choosing the Barlow Road through the Cascade Mountains, **Laurel Hill** needed to be descended. Previously described as the most difficult hill of the entire journey, it consisted of two right angle drops of 240 and 60 feet. With only 50 miles to the end, this hill was the last major obstacle to conquer.

Walter E. Meacham describes the hair-raising descent this way: ". . . Laurel Hill, a long, high, broken ridge about four miles in length. . . the oxen could not hold back the wagons, even when rough-locked. Some . . . took their wagons apart and slid them down . . . others cut trees and dragged them behind . . . others tied long ropes to the rear axle and wound one end around a tree, letting the rope out . . . (if) a rope broke, then there was a broken wagon to mend or abandon. The grooves worn on the trees by the ropes remained visible(even today - parentheses mine) as long as the trees stood." **93** Adding to this difficulty was the denseness of the Oregon forests. Trees and branches had to be cleared along this path before descending.

Mountain Peaks and Ranges

In most cases the pioneers avoided crossing mountains and traveled the lower elevation plains. That's one reason why the Trail usually stayed close to the rivers, since water always seeks the lowest level. However, two mountain ranges could not be avoided. The emigrants also saw other mountain peaks and ranges from a distance. Both contributed to the aesthetic quality of the journey.

Upon entering Wyoming the pioneers saw 10,000 foot **Laramie Peak** in the distance. They mistakenly thought it to be part of the Rocky Mountains, which they did not want to cross! Continuing through western Wyoming the jagged **Wind River Range** loomed to the north. These mountains provided a topographic contrast while the emigrants crossed the broad plateau through South Pass.

Only in Oregon did mountain ranges have to be crossed. West of Flagstaff Hill were the aptly named **Blue Mountains**, containing peaks close to 9,000 feet elevation. The pioneers tried to cross at passes much lower(around 4,000 feet). Even though these mountains provided abundant wood for fuel and animals for food, their danger lay with the possibility of early snows. For those taking the Barlow Road, delays through the "Blues" would also increase the chances for running into snow through the last mountains - the **Cascade Range**. Even though the latter mountains were not as high as the former, 4,000 feet high passes still needed to be crossed.

Probably the most inspirational part through these mountains was viewing **Mt. Hood**, Oregon's tallest mountain at 11,235 feet elevation. Its bright, white, pointed snowcap dwarfs all other Cascade peaks. The pioneers must have been awestruck - as was I - upon first seeing this majestic volcanic peak! I first encountered it at The Dalles, about 30 miles distant. Its white peak bathed by a bright, sunny, blue, cloudless sky took my breath away!

What is it about mountains that attract viewers? Why do many hikers climb mountains? "Because they are there," captures the spirit of risk-taking, adventure and challenge important to the pioneers and us today. The aesthetic quality of these landmarks was painted by the songwriter's phrase "purple mountains' majesty" in "America the Beautiful." The overused phrase "totally awesome" applies to these creations of Nature. Standing next to a mountain makes you seem insignificant in the scheme of things. Yet the Bible states we are created in the image of God. **94**

Spiritually, we associate mountains with reaching to the heavens. Greek and Roman mythology saw these peaks as places where the gods dwelt. The American Indians saw spirits dwelling in the mountains, making them sacred. Moses ascended Mt. Sinai to obtain the Ten Commandments directly from God. His was truly a "mountaintop experience." My life changing event came atop a mountain in Colorado when I asked Jesus Christ to come into my life and direct my "journey." Maybe you have you had a similar experience, although not necessarily on a mountain.

Mountains are seen as places of refreshment and peace. The poet Emmie Bohm, in "My Mountain Home", provides a vivid description:

"You ask me, my friend, where is my home
And where do I love to live and roam.
It is in the mountains, so rugged and high,
Where through the pines the summer winds sigh.

Where one wanders through the summer days
And gazes far into the shimmering haze.
Where faith is reborn and renewed are your hopes
As you listen to the birds' cheerful notes.

When you drink of the water, fresh and cool
Babbling crystal clear from a mountain pool.
Where you find tranquility and heavenly rest
Watching the sun go down in the west.

Where mountain flowers are blooming brighter
And the snow on the ranges stays longer, whiter.
Where you are contented, happy, and cheery
And peace is found for a heart which is weary.

There - Oh, friend - there is my home.
There's where I love to live and roam." **95**

Natural Bridge

One of the most idyllic settings along the Trail was **Ayers Natural Bridge** in eastern Wyoming. This 90 foot long natural red rock bridge with a stream underneath is the only one of its kind in the nation. Matthew C. Field describes this scene in 1843: ". . . to visit a remarkable mountain gorge - a natural bridge of solid rock, over a rapid torrent, the arch being regular as tho' shaped by art - 30 feet from base to ceiling, and 50 to the top of the bridge - wild cliffs, 300 feet perpendicular beetled above us, and the noisy current swept along among the huge fragments of rock at our feet." **96**

This was a favorite camping and resting spot for the emigrants. I enjoyed camping in the small, free county park marking this spot today. Listening to the soothing, bubbling stream was therapeutic for me. It's one way to totally relax by reading, hiking or simply enjoying this canyon off the beaten path. This place certainly has aesthetic value!

Landmarks In Our Lives

We have seen the importance of physical landmarks to the traveling pioneers, from lonely trees to majestic mountains. Hopefully you will notice these same signposts as you travel the Oregon Trail today. On a metaphorical level, what landmarks serve as turning points in our lives?

Many times we keep a hectic pace in our daily lives(remember the "tyranny of the urgent") and forget to mark important events in our lives. We need time to reflect upon their significance to us and others. This may mean a walk in the woods listening to the wind through the trees, strolling along the lake or ocean beach to the rhythm of the waves, or staring into a warm, crackling fire. The Psalmist exhorts us to "Cease striving and know that I am God." **97** We only need to take time to enjoy His Handiwork.

Just as landmarks indicated changes in scenery, so our landmarks usually indicate changes in our lives. They could be in the following four areas:

Physical - the process of growing from childhood to adulthood, including maturing and aging

Intellectual - the process of formal schooling from pre-school through graduate college, including becoming a lifelong learner

Social - the process of acquiring friends and a mate, raising children and adapting to the "empty nest"

Spiritual - the process of religious training through the home and church, including making your own commitments and acquiring a value system

We conveniently use decades to mark historical events. We refer to the Decade of the 1980s and 1990s. These ten year increments could be your landmarks to use in evaluating your life. One method would be to relate the above four areas by asking the following questions:

1. **Physical**

   In my life's "journey," am I progressing in my physical development? How physically fit am I?

2. **Social**

   In my life's "journey," am I progressing in my social development? Am I meeting my family's needs? Am I acquiring meaningful relationships? Am I reaching out to new friends?

3. **Intellectual**

   In my life's "journey," have I met the requirement for the degrees I want to achieve? Am I a lifelong learner, using my skills and abilities to pursue my "passion" areas?

4. **Spiritual**

In my life's "journey," have I satisfied my church's requirements for sacred observances?   Have I made a personal commitment to my God?   Do I know what values are important to me?

You may want to use a journal, or write in the margins of these pages, to record your answers to the questions in these four areas. Writing your thoughts can help clarify them. Hopefully, these questions will provide you with a start to periodically evaluate your life by using these landmarks. You may want to add others more specific to your situations. If you're camping along the Trail, a quiet time by the fire might start you on this reflective journey. Hopefully, these tangible pioneer landmarks will serve as guides for your intangible life's "journey."

The next lesson deals with another type of natural phenomena - the weather. The pioneers undoubtedly talked a lot about it but couldn't do much to control it. What can we learn from their experiences in dealing with these changes. Bring your hat, coat, boots and rainwear, and come along!

Lesson Seven

"Interpretive Center, Baker, OR

WEATHER: PREPARING FOR THE CHANGES

Remember the Great Midwest Flood of 1993? Our family certainly did! We lived in the largest American city(Des Moines, Iowa - population 200,000) to be without water. For twelve days we played pioneer. We used plastic containers of varying sizes to haul water from the National Guard trucks. We even found a place to shower without waiting in line for hours - a county park that still had water. This became our daily midnight bathing ritual. When the waters finally subsided, this "500 year flood" became the greatest natural disaster in American history.

During the Fall of 1992 the second most devastating natural disaster in the United States struck Florida and Louisiana in the form of Hurricane Andrew. Several weeks later another hurricane(Iniki) was the worst this century to hit the Hawaiian Islands. Both of these hurricanes packed winds up to 160 miles per hour with their torrential rains. What's going on?

During this same time period my home state of Iowa also experienced torrential rains up to sixteen inches in one dreadful night. Crops, rich topsoil, bridges and

101

roads were all washed away in the resultant flash flooding. The farmers needed the rain, but this was ridiculous! What's going on? Did the pioneers also experience these changes in weather conditions?

The above examples are extreme cases illustrating the negative impact these conditions can have on people's lives. One day your house and possessions are secure. The next day they're gone. Sounds like the Biblical parable cautioning against building your house on the sand. **98**

The pioneers didn't face anything this extreme. However, the changing weather conditions were always a consideration when traveling, especially since they were outside the entire time. Their only protection from the elements was inside their covered wagon and tents.

After distinguishing between **climate and weather**, this lesson will describe the types of weather experienced by the emigrants on the **plains and the mountains**. I will then speculate as to the ideal climate in which to reside. The influence of weather on personality will also be explored. I will visualize an ideal climate in which you may want to dwell.

Climate And Weather: What's The Difference?

In many parts of the United States we often hear the prediction, "If you want the weather to change, wait five minutes!" This is particularly true in the Midwest. Does this adage also apply to climate? What's the distinction between these terms?

Whereas - as the above saying correctly states - weather is changeable - climate is constant, even though the seasons change. Five geographic factors comprise the climatic conditions of an area: "water, latitude, elevation, prevailing winds and mountain ranges." **99** Which of these influences upon climate did the pioneers experience during their journey?

Even though **water** was essential to their travel, the rivers they stayed by were too small to affect the climate. However, the reason they settled in the Willamette Valley was influenced by the Pacific Ocean. Since water warms more slowly and cools more slowly than land, this rich agricultural area is cooler in the summer and warmer in the winter than land farther inland. This climate contributed to a longer growing season than the emigrants were used to in the Midwest. The stories of bountiful harvests in Oregon were true!

However, the pioneers journey was far away from the Pacific. Hence they experienced wide variations in temperature from spring to fall and during the day and nighttime hours.

The Oregon Trail was in a northwesterly direction. They started in Independence, Missouri(39 degrees North Latitude) and arrived in Oregon City(over 45 degree North Latitude, or half the distance between the Equator and the North Pole). Since one degree latitude represents approximately 70 miles north or south, the pioneers ended their journey close to 400 miles farther north than they started. Because of these **latitude** changes, they traveled through cooler temperatures than they were used to back home.

The third element of climate - **elevation** - played a significant part in the emigrants' "up and down" journey. Their jumping off point at Independence was approximately 800 feet elevation. They gradually climbed through Kansas, Nebraska and Wyoming to South Pass - elevation 7,550 feet. From this high point they descended until they encountered the mountain passes in Oregon. At their destination in Oregon City the elevation was under 100 feet.

A rule of thumb states that for every 1,000 feet of elevation gain the temperature decreases by 3.3 degrees Fahrenheit. Therefore the temperature at South Pass would be 22 degrees cooler than Independence. Conversely, Oregon City would be 25 degrees warmer than at

South Pass. Thus two places at the same latitude can experience a wide temperature variance due to elevation differences.

Prevailing winds influenced the weather patterns along the Trail. Since most weather patterns originate in the west and move east, the pioneers were usually traveling through new weather patterns - be it fair or foul. For example, a storm would affect emigrants in Oregon before reaching travelers in Nebraska. However, the skies would clear in the former place when the latter place would still be cloudy. Because of these winds over the Pacific Ocean, the climate on the West Coast in Oregon would be milder than farther inland like Nebraska. The "sword cuts both ways" because of the prevailing westerlies.

The fifth factor - mountain ranges - played an important role, especially when the pioneers traveled through Wyoming and Oregon. Remember the mountains I described as landmarks in the previous lesson. They served as barriers, not only for the journey, but also to alter the weather conditions from one side to the other. The western - or windward - side of the mountain is usually more moist. This is because the prevailing westerlies drops precipitation on the west side before climbing the mountain to the dry - or leeward - side. This phenomenon explains why the fields in Oregon(west of the Cascade Range) are green and fertile, whereas most of the Trail through eastern Oregon, Idaho, Wyoming and most of Nebraska are brown and barren. Today irrigation has made part of the "desert bloom," even though it is on the leeward side of the Blue and Rocky Mountains.

Map 2 depicts the major climatic regions of the United States. You can also see the Oregon Trail superimposed on these regions. You will notice the pioneers traveled through five distinct regions, from the very severe Great Interior to the mildest Pacific Coast. In between they encountered the rigorous Rocky Mountains, the arid Intermountain Plateau and the Cascades(the Sierra Nevadas were crossed by the users of the California Trail. As you travel the

Trail, be aware of these five factors and the five different climatic regions you are experiencing.

Now you can be the weatherperson on TV!

Map 2

Climatic Regions of the United States

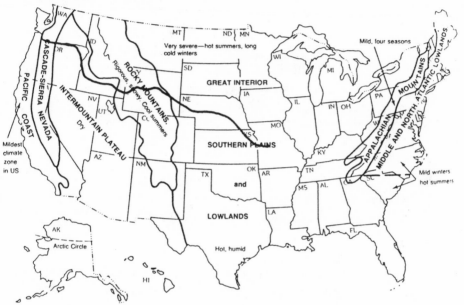

From Boyer & Savageau, <u>Places Rated Almanac</u>, 1989, p. 324.

Weather On The Plains

In keeping with the theme of changeability, the plains climate produced a variety of weather including thunderstorms, dust storms, searing heat in the daytime, followed by cool, humid nights.

Even though the emigrants experienced numerous **thunderstorms** in the Midwest, those on the plains were more spectacular. They seemed to come up suddenly from the west and created quite a production. The lightning was frightening and the thunder was deafening. It could literally rain bucketfuls in a short period of time.

The pioneers ran for shelter in their wagons or tents. Not so the oxen, horses and cattle. They couldn't hide. These thunderstorms could cause them to stampede. Rounding them up later in the mud was not fun! More lost time on the journey.

While traveling the Trail one summer, I experienced a severe summer thunderstorm similar to those encountered by the pioneers. While tenting in Grand Island, Nebraska, the western sky lit up with lightning, followed by crashing thunder. It rained nonstop that night a total of five inches. However, I was more fortunate than the pioneers. I spent most of the night in my Honda Civic - dry from the rain and protected from the lightning. But I didn't get much sleep!

Whether a particular year was abnormally dry or wet had a measurable impact upon the length of the emigrants' journey. For instance, both 1843 and 1844 were unseasonably moist. In the latter year heavy rains forced one wagon train to take two and a half weeks to ford one swollen stream. This same group needed sixty one days to travel 200 miles west of the Missouri River. **100** It would have been little surprise to the pioneers had they known today's National Severe Storm Center is located in Kansas City!

After the daytime rains the sun would come out with intensity, especially with no clouds. With moisture still in the air, the humidity would be high. This would also cause travel to be uncomfortable. As you can see by Map 3, the most humid portion of the Trail was from its origination in Independence to the panhandle of Nebraska(noontime average relative humidity of 41-50%).

Map 3

July Noon Average Relative Humidity

Over 60%
51–60%
41–50%
Under 40%

Source: National Oceanic and Atmospheric Administration, National Climatic Center

From Boyer & Savageau, <u>Places</u> <u>Rated</u> <u>Almanac</u>, 1989, p. 379.

The farther west they traveled, the drier the air. Wyoming, Idaho and Eastern Oregon comprised the most arid portion of the journey(humidity under 40%). Even though travel here was more comfortable, especially with less humid days and pleasantly cool nights, another problem emerged. The dry air would cause the emigrants' eyes to redden and their lips chapped and "puffed and cracked until just licking them was a torture. More serious was the effect on wood. (Wagon) wheels shrank; spokes and tires loosened(and fell off the rims). The need for repairs was constant." **101** These conditions didn't do much to boost their morale, even though they had less than one-third of their journey left.

The pioneers faced another new weather-related occurrence - dust storms. Because of the wide open spaces and scarcity of trees, these storms were more common than the emigrants experienced in their home states. A more arid climate(see Map 2) and higher average wind speed meant more dry topsoil "blowin' in the wind." For example, the average wind speed in Kansas City, Missouri is 10.3 miles per hour and its relative humidity at noon in July is 68%. Farther west, Casper, Wyoming experiences an average wind speed of 13 miles per hour and relative humidity of 56%. There is also a significant difference in elevation between the two cities - 1,000 for the former contrasted to over a mile high(5,300 feet) for the latter. **102** Remember the higher the elevation, the drier the air. Casper is on the leeward side of the Rockies - contributing to its dry climate. Because Casper is west of the 100th Meridian - the dividing line between the fertile and arid soil- it has fewer trees to keep the topsoil in place. Because of the above climatic factors, you can see why a dust storm is more likely in Casper than Kansas City.

As with the thunderstorms, the emigrants could not escape the sudden dust storms. The dirt would infiltrate their wagons and possessions. Difficulty of breathing was shared by both man and beast. At times the sky would be darkened, causing you to lose the Trail. Remember the "dust bowl" stories during the 1930s. The severity of the storms experienced by the pioneers were not like those during the Depression years. Instead they varied with the relative dryness or wetness of the year traveled.

I experienced a day on the Trail, 150 years later. In order to celebrate the 1993 sesquicentennial of the Great Emigration, a private company called the Oregon Trail Wagon Train allowed contemporary pioneers to ride or walk part of the Trail - for a fee. I chose the latter mode of transportation - for $29 a day you received three meals, a shower and all the dust you could eat!

After a hearty breakfast, we started promptly at 7:00 AM from the fairgrounds in Pendleton, Oregon. Our goal was to follow the original Trail as closely as possible. The first part of our journey found us walking along the shoulder of Interstate 84 - hardly an authentic walk. Finally we trekked along a blacktop road to our site for lunch - a farm surrounded by golden stalks of wheat gently blowing in the hot breeze.

Now the realism began. The next five miles was overland through the wheat fields - we made our own path. We walked single file - to avoid frightening the rattlesnakes(they're supposed to be more afraid of us than we of them)! The dust stirred up by the wagons, horses and hikers created a minute picture of what it must have been like with many more wagons on the Trail. We were even "treated" to a runaway wagon - not a staged event. After running for cover, a rider finally got the horses under control.

After continuing over hill and dale, and along a tranquil river, around 5:00 PM we finally reached our destination 26 miles later in Echo, Oregon. As my sore and blistered feet would attest, I experienced one day on the Trail. The pioneers did this repeatedly for almost six months! Now I can empathize somewhat with their plight!

Weather In The Mountains

The conditions the emigrants faced when crossing the mountain ranges were the opposite of those on the plains. Where the daytime heat bore down on them relentlessly through the "Great American Desert," the mountains - with their higher elevation - could produce numbing cold, especially at night. Instead of thunder-storms like those experienced on the plains, precipitation took the form of snow - and sometimes hail. Snow with wind equals blizzard - the biggest weather-related danger the pioneers faced in the mountains.

The gravest example of being unprepared during winter snows happened not on the Oregon - but the California - Trail. George and Jacob Donner were leading a wagon train of 87 emigrants from Illinois to California in

1846. **103** The Donner Party was behind schedule and decided to take a cutoff to make up time. In addition to this risk, they became trapped in the Sierra Nevada blizzards and deep snows during the winter of 1846-47. What subsequently happened is hard to believe! But it illustrates the importance of satisfying Maslow's basic needs(food and shelter).

Trapped in the snows throughout the winter, the party slowly faced starvation, illness, death and finally cannibalism - the living ate the dead to keep alive! In mid-January seven persons(two men and five women) managed to escape their "snow bound prison" and formed the first rescue party on February 19. The first stranded emigrant to see this party tearfully asked, "Are you men from California, or do you come from heaven?" As weather conditions permitted, three more rescue parties reached the remaining survivors during the next two months. The last expedition brought 47 persons out alive - slightly over half of the original party! **104**

The lesson learned from the above tragedy was stated succinctly by one of the survivors - thirteen-year-old Virginia Reed, ". . . never take no cutoffs and hury along as fast as you can, " **105** Today there is a monument at Donner Pass(north of Lake Tahoe in California) commemorating this disaster. "The mountains don't care" would be an appropriate sign to also place at this spot, as a warning to be prepared when traversing this difficult terrain.

Another weather occurrence in the mountains is hailstorms. Thunderstorms and lightning can accompany them. What may fall as rain in lower elevations condenses into round, icy, white pellets at the higher reaches. Generally the hail doesn't stay on the ground long, especially during the summer. Therefore it is not the hindrance to travel as is deep snow. However, it probably will send you running for cover!

I experienced a hailstorm in the mountains on one of my summer odysseys along the Trail. While camping in my tent at 6,000 feet elevation, I was awakened by the sound of a rushing wind(no, it wasn't Pentecost!) around 3:00 am. Then suddenly the tent reverberated with hundreds of direct hail hits. I looked outside and lo and behold the ground was white - in June! Thankfully, my tent and the tenter survived. It gave me the feeling the pioneers must have had on the Trail.

Even though I have dwelt on the negative weather changes, there were many pleasant days as well. The clear blue, sunny skies, followed by crisp, cool nights were invigorating, and no doubt provided psychological strength for the trip. The pink sunrises and sunsets over the plains were spectacular. The bright, starry nights in the mountains could remind the emigrants of the Creator's majestic work, if they would take the time to look up. The changing weather conditions brought variety to a mostly monotonous journey.

Searching For The Ideal Climate

The pioneers - like us today - could not control the weather. They had no Weather Channel or sirens to warn them of approaching storms. They had to face the changeable conditions as they traveled. As mentioned earlier in this lesson, the emigrants traveled through five climatic regions. Their destination in the Willamette Valley provided them with the mildest climate zone(Pacific Coast) in the nation. What do we think is the ideal climate in which to reside today? Is it also in Oregon? What criteria can we use to judge this subjective topic? We will search for these answers.

Places Rated Almanac(PRA) uses objective criteria to determine the mildest climate in the 333 metropolitan areas of the United States. "Mild" is defined as absence of extremes in temperatures, and is characterized by cool summers, warm winters, and long springs and autumns. Their ratings are based upon those areas "whose mean temperatures remain closest to 65 degrees Fahrenheit(considered by scientists as ideal for healthy living) for the greatest percentage of time." **106**

As Map 4 illustrates, three of the mildest climates are found in Oregon's Willamette Valley(Portland, Salem and Eugene-Springfield). As you can also see the emigrants had to travel through some of the most rigorous climate in Nebraska and Wyoming on the way to the "good climate." This rigorous climate receives low ratings from **PRA**. What does this say about the variety and changeableness of the weather most of us experience? May I suggest other criteria?

Map 4

Places Rated's Mildest and Wildest Metro Areas

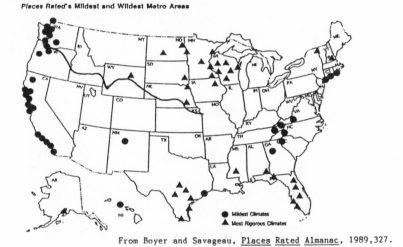

From Boyer and Savageau, <u>Places Rated Almanac</u>, 1989,327.

My objective criteria relates to the five geographic factors influencing climate(see earlier discussion in this lesson). According to my analysis, the ideal climate in the United States should consist of the following elements:

1. Within 100 miles of a major body of **water**(for moderation)

2. At a **latitude** indicating four distinct seasons(for variety)

3. At an **elevation** of at least 4,000 feet above sea level(less humid)

4. Within 100 miles of a **mountain range**(for aesthetic beauty))

5. Located on the leeward side of a mountain range(prevailing winds)

All of the mildest metro areas located on Map 4(PRA's "Mildest and Wildest Metro Areas") are eliminated by one or more of my specific criteria. The metro areas along the Eastern Coast and Gulf of Mexico do not benefit by their proximity to the Atlantic Ocean. Because the prevailing winds are westerly, they don't bring a moderating effect to these areas from the Atlantic Ocean. The Appalachian areas are more than 100 miles from the Atlantic Ocean.

The Western Coast areas of Southern California on Map 4 do not experience four distinct seasons. The Northern California, Oregon and most Washington metro areas are located on the windward side of mountain ranges. This causes their climates to be rainy and cloudy. The only exception to this is Yakima, which is more than 100 miles from the Pacific Ocean.

Therefore all these metro areas on both coasts don't meet all five of my criteria. They are all under 4,000 feet elevation as well. The only mild metro area above 4,000 feet is Albuquerque, New Mexico - much more than 100 miles from an ocean. Where else is the ideal climate? It can be found in the mountainous rural areas of the three Western Coastal states.

The State of Washington has the Olympic Peninsula on the Pacific Ocean. The climate on the eastern side of the Olympic Mountains is much drier and sunnier than the rain forest on the western side of this mountain barrier. East of Puget Sound and the Cascade Range lies another ideal four-season climate. Living on the leeward side of the Cascade Range in northern and central Oregon would be another ideal area. Living in Northern California(north of Eureka) on the east side of one of the many mountain ranges(Siskiyou, Klamath, Marble, Salmon, Scott Bar, Scott, and Trinity) would also meet my criteria - provided you lived no lower than 4,000 feet elevation in any of the above areas. Sounds like a cabin in the mountains may be an ideal place to live!

Even though these ideal areas are not on the Oregon Trail, you could visit them after reaching the end of the Trail at Oregon City. You could head north to Washington and/or south to Northern California. Maybe you'll find these areas to be the ideal climate also. Remember, this is my subjective opinion, based on the above criteria. Your tastes may vary!

The Willamette Valley where most of the pioneers settled lies to the west of the Cascade Range in Oregon. Since this is on the windward side, this is not the ideal climate according to my criteria. It's excellent for the crops but it may rain too much for the people's mental health. There may a link between depression and a cloudy, rainy climate. With tongue-in-cheek Oregonians describe the weather in this part of their state: "It only rains once a year - it starts in October and ends in May!"

Visualizing The Ideal Climate

In addition to the above objective analysis, there is also a subjective aspect to this aesthetic subject of climate. Remember this is Maslow's highest level of human needs. By using the imaginative right side of your brain, you can visualize your ideal climate.

Color is another important aspect of climate. I have concluded the ideal climate should be predominantly composed of at least four bright colors in each of four distinct seasons. Thus my **"four by four" colortherapy climatic** model. The clear **blue** sky with the **yellow** sun shining on the **green** pine trees and the **white** snow paints an idyllic winter scene(four colors). In the spring the white, pink and purple buds of the deciduous trees would add color to a clear sky and bright sun(five colors). In the autumn these same trees, with their shades of gold, orange and red add vibrancy to the season(five colors). The summer would have only three colors - even with a bright blue sky - since the trees would be green. Summer in the mountains could add a fourth color - if you could see snowcaps. An area with mainly gray, cloudy skies and brown trees and terrain(two colors) does not contain as much aesthetic beauty as the "big four" colors.

To give you an impression of how the scenery would appear, visualize spending a day in the ideal climate. Please participate in the following exercise by following these directions. You may want to first set the mood by playing soft background music such as the natural sounds of a surging ocean, babbling brook or peaceful forest. Assume a comfortable position on the floor or soft chair and close your eyes. If possible, request that someone else read the following directions and descriptions to you, allowing time to pause after each set of ellipsis. "Breathe deeply and slowly allow your body to relax. . . Let all the tension flow out of your body. . . Relax. . . With each breath, you are allowing your body to become lighter, to expand, to slowly become all of the air in the room. . . Gently let yourself rise slowly above the room . . ." **107**

"Imagine you are living in a cozy cabin nestled in the **green** Pondersa Pines of the Cascade Mountains in Oregon. Your dwelling place is located at an elevation of 5,000 feet on the leeward side of these mountains. You wake up to the birds in the forest. What do they sound like? . . . You arise to see the bright **yellow** sun in a cloudless **blue** sky. Take time to enjoy these bright colors and to wake up. . . . You notice the fresh **white** snow that has fallen during the night, and the sun's reflection on it. Realize how these colors are energizing you for the day's tasks. . . You put on the coffee, get dressed and eat breakfast. Is someone with you in the house, or are you by yourself? . . .Notice the smells emanating from your solar-heated kitchen. . . . You then take your coffee outside on the deck for a period of meditation, prayer and thanksgiving for the beautiful day. What are you thinking about? How do you feel? . . .

You are now ready to start your work for the day. Will you be staying in your cabin, or walking or driving someplace else? . . . What will the scenery at your workplace be like? . . . Will it have the same colors as those surrounding your cabin? . . . What type of work are you doing? . . . With whom are you interacting? . . . Do you enjoy your work? . . . Do you feel a sense of accomplishment and satisfaction in what you are doing today? . . .

You have finished your work for the day. Do you walk or drive back to your cabin, or have you been home all day? . . . Does someone meet you at home? . . . Who is it?. . . What are you preparing for supper? Do you dine with someone else, or alone? . . . After supper you go outside for a walk in the woods. Notice the shadows on the trees and snow and the sun setting in the west. . . How does it look? . . . After your walk you go back inside the cabin. You curl up in front of a crackling fire with a good book. What are you reading? . . . You then prepare for bed. How do you feel at the end of the day? . . .

When you are ready, slowly allow yourself to drift back to your room. Notice how you feel. . . . When you are ready open your eyes. Then share your experiences with someone else or record them in your journal."

Hopefully the above experience created a mental picture of the importance of color in influencing your attitude during this day. These four colors would seem to make your day more vibrant and invigorating. Plentiful sunshine can be an antidote to depression. An opposite condition called SAD(Seasonal Affective Disorder) can result from a prolonged deficiency of sunshine, especially during the winter months in northern latitudes. A technique called light therapy, whereby a person lies by a bank of lights or is exposed to natural sunlight, is used to combat this common psychological problem.

I am suggesting a novel type of treatment - **colortherapy**. A person suffering from depression in a climate where less than four colors are dominant would spend time in a "four by four" climate. Isn't this what travel agencies encourage - "snowbirds"going South for the winter? This prescription would assume other conventional means of treatment(psychological and spiritual) did not work. A vacation to the green forested and white snowcapped mountains, or to a blue lake or ocean, or traveling to an arid climate with much sunshine may be in order. Possibly a permanent move to one of these areas would be needed. I realize depression can have many causes, but this therapy may help alleviate it. It may be worth a try. Who knows, maybe this will become a new science! Remember, you read it first here!

Lessons From The Changeable Weather

We have seen the pioneers experiencing both adverse and pleasant weather conditions. We have seen people today subjected to natural disasters while others live in a mild and nonthreatening climate. What can we learn from these observations?

First, weather - related disasters remind us of man's powerlessness and God's awesomeness. **Second**, the same God that allows disasters also brings sunshine, rain and pleasant weather. **Third**, we should adopt the attitude of the Biblical character Job who - after he had been subjected to tragedies - made two conclusions, "I came naked from my mother's womb and I shall have nothing when I die. The Lord gave me everything I had, and they were his to take away. Blessed be the name of the Lord" and "Shall we receive only pleasant things from the hand of God and never anything unpleasant?" **108 Fourth**, a partial cure for depression may be living in a climate with more color(colortherapy). **Fifth**, the ideal climate is located in parts of the three West Coast states.

Keeping the above lessons in mind might enrich your journey as you travel through changeable weather.

Have a nice, sunny day!

Our journey will now take us into the human element to discuss the importance of depending upon each other. What lessons can we learn from these pioneer families?

"Oregon Trail Wagon Train, Bayard, NE"

FAMILY, FRIENDS AND INDIANS: DEPENDING
UPON EACH OTHER

Our journey thus far has emphasized Maslow's lower needs and Aristotle's limited real goods(Refer to Diagrams 1 and 2 in Lesson Two). The pioneers needed to take ample supplies(Lesson Two) and find adequate water sources(Lesson Four). They also needed the knowledge furnished by reliable guides and guidebooks(Lesson Three). The protection offered by forts and missions(Lesson Five), and from the changing weather(Lesson Seven), satisfied their safety needs.

Several of the lessons have dwelt on Maslow's higher levels and Artistotle's unlimited real goods. A prerequisite of taking the risk to travel to Oregon was a positive self-concept(Lesson One). Once on the Trail the pioneers did enjoy the aesthetic beauty(Lesson Six).

This lesson will concentrate on Maslow's higher need for belonging and love, and Aristotle's unlimited real good of friendship. The trek to Oregon was a group experience that demanded cooperation from family and friends in a wagon train. Assistance from outside the "trains" was provided by friendly Indians, "roadside telegraphs" and "gobacks."

On this leg of our journey we will address the following questions: How did the pioneers cooperate to achieve their goals? How did they depend on each other to meet each other's needs? How did they divide the responsibilities of the trip? What abilities did they utilize?

Following the book's contemporary application, we will address the issues of family cooperation and division of responsibility today. The importance of friends and neighbors will also be explored. Finding and utilizing your gifts and talents to benefit others and yourself will be addressed. Finally, the role of stereotypes, vis-a-vis Native Americans, will be discussed.

Cooperation Within The Wagon Train

Two thousand miles with the same people - family and new friends. Sounds exciting at first. But like college roommates, you discover each other's idiosyncrasies after living together awhile. You must remember your common purpose to reach the "good life" in Oregon. The higher mission and calling needs to override individual differences. Hence the need for cooperation.

How did the pioneers cooperate for a successful journey? The main method was making sure everyone shared in the responsibilities of the trip. Men, women and children all performed specific duties based on their traditional roles. The men were responsible for protecting the people from unfriendly Indians and wild animals. They had ready access to their rifles during the day. The night saw a rotating guard shift in operation. Men rounded up the oxen, horses and cattle each morning, drove them on the Trail and corralled them at night. After the guide determined the best route for the day, several of the men used picks and shovels to smooth the "road." Needed repairs on the wagons and equipment were performed by the males.

Once the guide had determined the campsite for the night, the women were responsible for setting up tents that evening and breaking camp the following morning. They also prepared the meals and washed the dishes afterwards. Washing and mending clothes was another duty.

The children fed the animals and assisted in readying them for each day's journey. The young people gathered firewood and their favorite fuel - "buffalo chips!" This latter smelly fuel burned well, and was plentiful on the plains where the trees were sparse. The children managed to entertain themselves with their own games and harmless diversions.

The above responsibilities assumed men and women were proficient in their respective duties. The men were considered more mechanically and physically adept. The women exhibited caring and domestic abilities. The children could be creative in the types of games they played.

What if there were exceptions to the above stereotypes? A woman might be better at repairing a wagon, whereas a man might be a creative cook. In these cases, who did what? Probably tradition(remember "Fiddler on the Roof.") prevailed. This may mean the wagons would break down more often and the food may be burned! There could be another way of handling these exceptions - each person using her or his talents for the good of the wagon train.

Cooperation Within Families Today

Today's families are not as traditional as those 150 years ago. Not only are the roles blurred, but the family unit itself is radically different from those in the wagon trains. The typical pioneer family lived on the farm with both spouses staying home to divide the responsibilities. The father mainly worked outside in the fields while the mother tended to the household and child-rearing tasks. Today this traditional family - though urban instead of rural - comprises only 7% of America's population. **109** Now over 50% of all mothers with pre-school age children are working outside the home. How do these changes affect the family roles?

Time becomes more important than role in today's

families. With the mother home less, someone has to pick up the slack - and the clothes! The father and the children can do the cooking, wash the dishes, wash and iron the clothes and clean the house. If this fails, there is always the cleaning lady! Availability is more important than aptitude in these situations. What if the latter were more important than the former attribute?

Assessing Our Talents

Family members would then be recognized as individuals possessing various God-given gifts and talents, respective of gender. The goal would be to determine a person's strengths and match them with an important family task. I will describe two contemporary methods to facilitate this process.

Diagram 4

What Skills You Have and Most Enjoy Using

Generally speaking, all skills divide into six clusters or families. To see which ones you are *attracted to*, try this PARTY exercise:
Below is an aerial view of a room
in which a two-day (!) party is taking place.
At this party, people with the same or similar interests have (for some reason) all gathered in the same corner of the room —
as described below:

(R) **1**
People who have athletic or mechanical ability, prefer to work with objects, machines, tools, plants, or animals, or to be outdoors.

2 (I)
People who like to observe, learn, investigate, analyze, evaluate, or solve problems.

(C) **6**
People who like to work with data, have clerical or numerical ability, carrying things out in detail or following through on other's instructions.

The Party

People who have artistic, innovating or intuitional abilities, and like to work in unstructured situations, using their imagination or creativity.
3 (A)

People who like to work with people — influencing, persuading or performing or leading or managing for organizational goals or for economic gain.

People who like to work with people—to inform, enlighten, help, train, develop, or cure them, or are skilled with words.

(E) **5**

4 (S)

1
Which corner of the room would you instinctively be drawn to, as the group of people you would most *enjoy* being with for the longest time? (leave aside any question of shyness, or whether you would have to talk with them.) Write the *letter* for that corner

2
After fifteen minutes, everyone in the corner you have chosen, leaves for another party cross-town, except you. Of the groups *that still remain* now, which corner or group would you be drawn to the most, as the people you would most *enjoy* being with for the longest time? Write the letter for that corner

3
After fifteen minutes, this group too leaves for another party, except you. Of the corners, and the groups, which remain now, which one would you most enjoy being with for the longest time? Write the letter for that corner

The first method of assessing your interests and abilities is based on the work of John Holland. He classifies all skills into six clusters or families. Try the exercise called "The Party"(see Diagram 4) to find the people with which you feel most comfortable. You may find your "people" will be all on one side of this hexagon - either the left or the right.

The second method of determining your aptitude relates to the pioneering(not to be confused with the emigrants!) work of contemporary Harvard professor Howard Gardner. His **Frames of Mind** divided human intelligences into the following seven broad categories:

Linguistic(verbal ability with words)
Musical(sensitivity to melody, rhythm and tone)
Logical-mathematical(perceives patterns, relationships and abstractions)
Spatial(perceives the visual world accurately)
Bodily-Kinesthetic(ability to use the body and to work skillfully with objects)
Interpersonal(capacity to relate well and lead others)
Intrapersonal(capacity to understand and act upon one's own feelings)

More recently Dr. Gardner has speculated on an additional type of intelligence - spiritual. At a conference on talent development in Iowa City, Iowa, I had the chance to ask Mr. Gardner about this claim. He believes certain people, such as the Dalai Lama and Mohandas Gandhi, are attuned to the invisible world of the metaphysical. However, Gardner was careful to distinguish the spiritual from the religious.

One inventory(see Appendix) allows you to apply Gardner's multiple intelligences. It was developed by Frank Rainey, State Consultant for Gifted and Talented Education in the Colorado Department of Gifted Education. By following the directions for the statements, you can obtain a comprehensive view of your strengths and weaknesses. As in the above two assessments, you must be honest and objective. Socrates' admonition "Know thyself" is applicable in these exercises. Even the ability to understand yourself shows an aptitude in **intrapersonal intelligence** - one of Gardner's categories.

Even though the pioneers didn't have access to these self-inventories, they exercised most of the above abilities. Those writing diaries and journals needed linguistic talents. Musical talent may have been evident as a means of relaxing at the end of the day. Those who kept track of expenditures were using their logical-mathematical abilities. Persons building or repairing wagons exercised spatial abilities. Bodily-kinesthetic skills were very important for the many physical and mechanical tasks. Leadership talents of the guides would exhibit interpersonal ability. They probably didn't have time to reflect and analyze their feelings along the journey(intrapersonal). This would come after they had settled in Oregon.

Utilizing Our Talents

Do we utilize our talents in our families today? If you have taken one or all of the inventories provided in this book, you undoubtedly have identified your interests and abilities. Now the goal is to build upon these strengths and match them with your household tasks.

The person skilled at logical-mathematical reasoning could formulate a budget and keep track of the checkbook. If this person is also adept at working with data, a computer could be used for tracking the budget and figuring taxes. The member skilled in spatial relationships who enjoys working with objects could be the builder and repairer. Another adult or child talented with objects could perform the bulk of the cooking. Washing the dishes and cleaning the house takes another type of skill with objects. A member with intrapersonal skills could create a vision and set goals with the entire family. The talented interpersonal leader could motivate the others to work together to accomplish these goals.

Another method of determining abilities is to see which roles are taken by family members performing a holiday program for family gatherings. First the organizer(good with people - interpersonal) determines responsibilities. Carols are sung or played(musical). The Christmas or Hanukkah story is read from the Bible(linguistic). Someone may have composed an appropriate poem(linguistic). A speech may be given relating the importance of the season(linguistic-intrapersonal). Many talents - some of which may be hidden the rest of the year - are uncovered in this setting.

You may have noticed in the above examples I didn't assume certain roles would be performed by males or females. Duties based on ability and interest would be implemented more cheerfully than those stereotyped by gender. With the majority of women working outside of the home today, identifying and utilizing your talents is more important than during the traditional pioneer era. I encourage you to try this approach in managing your household.

Utilizing Our Time

Another difference between the emigrant families and those of today is the amount of time spent together. The former families were always together when traveling. They worked, ate and slept together. This sounds like a virtue today, but this closeness undoubtedly caused problems. Little irritants could become a bigger problem than needed.

Many of today's families have a dearth of time to spend with each other. One of the best times to communicate is at mealtime. According to a 1990 survey, "seventy percent of American parents have dinner at home with their children at least five times per week." **110** However, other people quoted in this survey were lucky if their families ate together three times per week. Meals today seem to revolve around the parents' work schedules and the childrens' activities. There's no certain time for meals anymore. When I was growing up the town siren blew at 12 noon and 6:00 PM - signifying mealtimes. The "tyranny of the urgent" undermines our time together. Quality time is further eroded if we eat together while watching that passive entertainer - the "tube." How can we provide more quality and quantity time for our families?

One way is to set aside a weekly family night when everyone stays home. Establish the following rules:

1. No interruptions for phone calls(screen calls with your answering machine).

2. Don't answer the door unless you are expecting someone.

3. Turn off the TV during this time.

4. Use your identified abilities(discussed in this lesson) to plan a program, using a variety of activities(board games, stories, music, reading, sharing or going out together).

5. Use your creativity!

Stephen Covey, in **The Seven Habits Of Highly Effective People,** explains how we can effectively utilize our time. His Time Management Matrix(see Diagram 5) depicts four quadrants using two variables defining time usage - urgency(requires immediate attention) and importance(concerned with results). Quadrant I, since it is both **urgent** and **important**, requires immediate attention. This is where crises and problems develop. Quadrant III activities are **urgent but not important**, although they seem to be the latter. Because of the tyranny of the urgent, most of our time spent in these quadrants is reactive in nature. **111**

Diagram 5   THE TIME MANAGEMENT MATRIX

	Urgent	Not Urgent
Important	I ACTIVITIES: Crises Pressing problems Deadline-driven projects	II ACTIVITIES: Prevention, PC activities Relationship building Recognizing new opportunities Planning, recreation
Not Important	III ACTIVITIES: Interruptions, some calls Some mail, some reports Some meetings Proximate, pressing matters Popular activities	IV ACTIVITIES: Trivia, busy work Some mail Some phone calls Time wasters Pleasant activities

From Covey, The Seven Habits of Highly Effective People, 1989, 151.

Quadrant IV activities are **neither urgent nor important**. This is where individuals can waste time watching television or doing other trivial activities. Quadrant II activities are **important but not urgent**. As such it is easy to procrastinate and not delve into such tasks as writing a mission statement, defining long-range goals, building lasting relationships, exercising and preventing Quadrant I problems from occurring. According to Covey the essence of effective personal management is to emphasize Quadrant II activities over the other three. **112** How can you do this with today's harried, hurried family?

Covey's answer is to put first things first by writing a mission statement for yourself, your family and your vocation. Then you can develop a weekly planner relating roles, goals and schedules. Your activities should be correlated with the roles you play at home(husband, father, wife, mother, son or daughter), work (manager or employee), church (teacher), school (student) or the community (volunteer). Short-term goals should be established for each role(See example in Diagram 6). Your priorities for the week can then be scheduled. If your activities don't relate back to your mission in life and aren't the Quadrant II type, you need to de-emphasize them in favor of effectively using your time.

Even though this process takes time initially, the end result should be to spend more time doing important activities with your family. The emphasis is on quality time. The pioneers had a mission - to obtain the "good life" by completing the journey to Oregon. What's the mission for yourself, your family and your vocation? I encourage you to try this approach to effective time management.

Cooperation Outside The Wagon Trains

Many diaries, journals and books portray the activities of one wagon train. They do not emphasize the emigrant interaction with other travelers. From 1849 to 1853 trails became congested with many wagons and crowded campsites. Reuben Knox observed 1,000 wagons passing Fort Kearny on the last day of May 1850. **113** As George Donner expressed in 1846: "Our journey has not been as solitary as we feared. . . Several companies are just ahead." **114** There was much opportunity for cooperation - and occasionally friction and flaring tempers from too much togetherness.

Interaction ranged from satisfying the lower to the higher level needs of Maslow's and Aristotle's hierarchies(see Diagrams 1 and 2 in Lesson Two). John Unruh's **The Plains Across** provides many examples of these humanitarian acts. The most significant assistance rendered was giving or selling provisions such as **food, water, blankets and clothing.** Fresh milk and butter from the traveling cows, and liquor were popular items for sale. Emigrants who recently crossed a dry area sometimes furnished "water wagons" to assist their counterparts across this treacherous territory. **115**

The role of **physicians** on the journey was particularly important. These services were first rendered by Dr. Marcus Whitman during the Great Migration of 1843. Doctors were invaluable in giving advice and dispensing medicine for the dreaded cholera - especially east of Fort Laramie. Companies without a doctor maneuvered to keep close to a "train" with a physician on board. **116**

Diagram 6   From <u>The</u> <u>Seven</u> <u>Habits</u> <u>of</u> <u>Highly</u> <u>Effective</u>

The WEEKLY WORKSHEET™	Week of:	Sunday	Monday
Roles — **Goals**	**Weekly Priorities**	**Today's Priorities**	

Roles	Goals	Weekly Priorities	Sunday	Monday
				(16) Salary Review Report
Individual– Personal Devel.	Rough draft mission statement (1); Register seminar (2); Visit Frank in hospital (3)			
Husband / Father	Home mgmt./Karla's class (4); Tim's science project (5); Sarah's bike (6)			
			Appointments/Commitments	
Manager– New Products	Test market parameters (7); Interv. ass't candidates (8); Study consumer survey (9)		8 (1) Private Time; 9 Mission State–	8; 9
Manager– Research	Study last test result (10); Work on bonding prob. (11); Network with Ken and Peter (12)		10 ment; 11; 12	10; 11 (8) Assistant Job; 12 Interviews
Manager– Staff Devel.	Performance review with Janie (13); Visit with Samuels (14)		1; 2	1; 2
Manager– Administration	End of month reports (15); Salary review report (16)		3; 4; 5	3; 4 (3) Frank–Hospital; 5
United Way Chairman	Prepare agenda (17); P.R. visit with Conklin (18); Start next year's plan (19)		6; 7; 8	6; 7 (6) Sarah's Bike; 8
			Evening	Evening

SHARPEN THE SAW

Physical _____

Mental _____

Spiritual _____

Social/Emotional _____

Tuesday	Wednesday	Thursday	Friday	Saturday
Today's Priorities				
②Send in seminar registration	⑫Ken Peter		⑭ Visit Samuels	
Appointments/Commitments				
8	8	8	8	8 Home mgmt. ④ Karla's class
9	9 ⑦ Test market	9 ⑪ Bonding	9 ⑩ Test results	9
10	10 parameters	10 problem	10 study	10
11	11	11	11	11
12	12	12	12 ⑱ Conklin	12
1 ⑨ Study consumer	1	1	1	1
2 survey	2	2	2	2
3	3	3 ⑬ Performance	3 ⑮ EOM report	3
4	4	4 review-Janie	4	4
5	5	5	5	5
6 ⑤ Tim's project	6	6 ⑰ United Way	6	6
7	7	7 agenda	7	7
8	8	8 ⑲Next yrs. plans	8	8
Evening	Evening	Evening	Evening	Evening 7:00 Theater– Browns

Emigrants helped each other in many other ways. Securing working wagon equipment by purchasing or trading for replacement parts was essential. Passing overlanders who pulled wagons from mudholes were appreciated. Searching for stray animals was a common act of cooperation. Toward the end of the journey some of the animals gave out or were stolen or killed by Indians. Pioneers unable to transport their belongings sometimes arranged for other overlanders to carry their supplies free or for a fee. A more unusual and less joyous task was digging and marking graves for deceased emigrants. 117

A higher level of need was the sharing of **information** among strangers encountered along the Trail. During each year of the migration a small percentage of emigrants(usually less than two percent) turned back and returned to the East. Some of these "gobacks" - in order to justify their own failure to reach the "good life" in Oregon - exaggerated the problems of cholera, insufficient grass and Indian attacks. Others did return because of the above problems, personal injury, company quarrels or homesickness. Nevertheless, they shared valuable information on trail conditions and cutoffs, the availability and prices of supplies at forts and trading posts, whether ferries were available to ford rivers, and the locations of buffalo herds. They even carried the mail eastward - a reverse slow Pony Express! However, the main contribution of these "turn-arounds" may have been the emotional and psychological boost they gave to the westbound travelers with their stories of the fertile fields in Oregon. These optimists were traveling west to bring their families to the promised land. "What further proof could anyone need that utopia[the"good life"]] was just across the mountains, and that those mountains could be crossed." 118

The "**roadside telegraph**" or "**bone express**" was an effective means of communicating with friends, relatives and fellow emigrants following along the Trail. This crude procedure involved writing a message on paper, trees, wood, rocks, animal bones or even human skulls, and attaching them to trees, rocks or grave markers along the Trail. The messages were of two types: (1) for specific individuals or wagon trains or (2) general information concerning the conditions ahead. The former were removed when the appropriate person learned the condition of their friends or relatives ahead of them The latter type stayed in their original places to benefit others. They cautioned of bad grass and water and possible Indian threats while directing pioneers to fresh springs or the last available water before crossing the desert. While generally accurate this "post office" also accentuated rumors of Indian massacres and grass and water shortages. This information was an important aspect of emigrant cooperation. **119**

One of the most common means of interaction along the Trail was the spontaneous **visits** among wagon trains. This face-to-face communication usually occurred at mealtimes, nights or on rest days(usually Sundays). When traveling during the day many emigrants rode ahead, lagged behind or wandered from their wagon trains to hunt, explore, fix a wagon, read, sketch a picture, visit and sometimes sleep. Because they didn't return to their companies in time, they sometimes shared a meal or spent the night with fellow travelers. Worshipping together at religious services on Sunday, or while resting in close proximity, provided another means of making new friends and engaging in conversation. **120**

Cooperation Among Friends and Neighbors Today

The above examples of interaction among the emigrants were needed to successfully complete their journey. They cooperated from necessity to achieve a common goal in Oregon. How do we interact with our friends and neighbors today? Do we base cooperation on necessity, or is it at the higher levels of Maslow's love and belonging or Aristotle's friendship?

Today our basic needs for **food, water and clothing** are met by a trip to the store - usually a short journey. People used to borrow a cup of sugar or an egg from their neighbors to continue baking. With the proliferation of 24 hour grocery and convenience stores(do we really need another

"Quick Trip" or "Seven Eleven?"), this practice has become obsolete. Maybe it also is a reflection of not knowing our neighbors well. However, we might borrow our neighbor's ladder or hedge trimmer(probably not necessities), and hopefully remember to return it.

Adequate **medical care** is certainly a necessity. Even today more than thirty million Americans are without health insurance. The 1992 Presidential election campaign focused on policies to contain health care costs and expand coverage. Maybe the Clinton Administration will take steps to control these spiraling costs and provide more affordable health care for everyone.

In the recent past the physician made house calls with his black bag(today only used in medical school). Now we visit the doctor at neighborhood clinics. If further treatment is needed, a comprehensive hospital using the latest diagnostic high tech equipment is available. Regional trauma centers and helicopter transports are available in emergency situations. The pioneers would be amazed if they could witness this progress in the medical field.

Do we have **"go-backs" and "turn-arounds"** today? What about individuals and families who move from one geographic location to another in the United States in search of their "good life?" Remember one of Naisbitt's megatrends - the irreversible migration from the North and East to the South and West. Even though this pattern is still occurring, we are seeing people moving back to their roots.

Witness the current situation in California. For millions this was the land of opportunity. Pack your belongings and surfboard and head West, seeking your fortune(good job) and fame(the influence of Hollywood)! This sounds similar to the motivations of the original "gold rushers" of 1849. As a result, the population of the "Golden State" grew 26% from 1980-1990. California's population of over thirty million now exceeds the entire country of Canada. 121 But then something unexpected happened. The end of the Cold War caused cutbacks in military contracts and bases, especially in Southern California. This severe recession caused people to relocate back to the Midwest and other areas where they were raised. For the first time net outmigration became greater than immigration. As a result, these modern "gobacks" could share firsthand experiences of the positive and negative aspects of pursuing the "American Dream" in California.

With instantaneous communication today(satellite television) the stories told by those living in one part of the country can be readily seen and heard everywhere in the United states. We don't have to wait days and weeks for information, as did the pioneers. However, when driving in stormy weather we may seek the advice of a trucker who has recently traveled where we are headed. These modern "turnarounds" may be a more up-to-date source of weather information than our radio.

Yesterday's **"roadside telegraph"** has been replaced by the post office and electronic mail. However, we still see graffiti displayed in restrooms and public places(bridges and walls). Maybe this illustrates another of Naisbitt's megatrends - moving from forced technology to high tech/high touch. . . . "whenever new technology is introduced into society, there must be a counterbalancing human response - that is, high touch - or the technology is rejected. The more high tech, the more high touch." **122** As we use more computers, modems and fax machines, we will need more handwritten notes. How many of us have a computer at our desk but always carry the sticky "post it" pads with us - for a personal touch?

How important is **visiting** with friends, neighbors and relatives today? Are we spending too much time in Quadrants I, III and IV activities(see Diagram 5 above) to participate in building relationships(Quadrant II activity)? **Three factors** in the last 40 years have impeded this form of communication.

First is the prevalence of television in the home. According to A.C. Nielsen Research, 98 percent of American households own at least one TV set, and the average viewing time is approximately 20 hours per week. **123** It's difficult to conduct a meaningful dialogue against the noise of the "tube". Here conversation tends to revolve around the program you are watching or utterances during the commercials. Persons who have removed the television permanently, or turned it off for a week or more, experienced an increase in stimulating discussions, reading and playing board games. They moved from passive to active interaction like the pioneers.

Second is the use of room and central air conditioners in homes in the humid climates of the United States(East, Midwest and South). How did people cool off at night before this invention? They probably sat on their front porch and conversed with their neighbors. Now we stay inside and watch television - both inhibiting conversation.

Designers and developers are trying to reverse this isolation. Houses are again being built with front porches. Many neighborhoods are utilizing more walking paths and greenbelts. Some cities are even designating certain sections only for pedestrian traffic. Maybe these changes will assist us to meaningfully communicate again. Remember Naisbitt's balance between high tech and high touch.

Third is the plethora of "latchkey" children - due to the prevalence of working women. Today these daughters and sons come home from school to a house devoid of humans, but probably containing a cat or dog. Mother is not there to greet them with a hug and a plate of freshly-baked cookies and cold milk. This was usually the time she would ask how their day was. Hopefully an answer more elaborate than "fine" would follow. This could be a special time to communicate before watching television, playing or doing homework. Today this "precious moment" is generally gone.

Today visiting is more apt to take place while driving to lessons, soccer and softball games, or shopping at the grocery store or the mall. The conversation is likely to be short and to the point. More relaxed sharing may ensue when eating out as a family. This is a time to forget about hectic schedules and share dreams and goals together.

Visiting takes time to share our thoughts and feelings with another person. As a child I remember going with my father to visit his father. They would sit in the dark(I would usually be "snooping" in an adjacent room) and talk about the weather("How much rain did we get last night?"), the crops("The corn looks good this year.") and the local news("Did you hear about the accident north of town?"). Between each subject a long period of silence would follow. Even though the conversation was at a surface level, they took the time to interact. This ingredient seems to be needed in today's society.

Aristotle and the Bible on Friendship

Aristotle's **Nicomachean Ethics** devotes two books to a discussion of friendship. He deals with (1) the need for friends (2) kinds of friendship (3) true friendship and (4) the number of friends needed. Solomon's Biblical Books of Proverbs and Ecclesiastes contain several pertinent references to friendship. How do these authors' depictions of friendship relate to the pioneers? to your friends?

Even though friendship is derived outside of oneself - as are physical goods and wealth - Aristotle classifies friendship as an unlimited real good instead of a limited external good(Refer to Diagram 2). Friendship is as important as goods acquired from within - self-esteem, knowledge and aesthetic beauty. "For without friends no one would choose to live, though he had all other goods[limited and unlimited real goods] . . . for with friends men are more able both to think and to act. . . for no one would choose the whole world on condition of being alone, since man is a political creature[animal] and one whose nature is to live with others." **124** Solomon sees friendship as synergistic when he concludes: "Two can accomplish twice as much as one, for the results can be much better." **125**

Aristotle sees three kinds of friendships. One type loves for the sake of what is **useful** for him. Another loves because of what is **pleasant** for herself. These friendships are only incidental and last only as long as one person derives utility or pleasure from the relationship. The pioneers relied on the utilitarian type of friends to accomplish the tasks described earlier in this chapter. You no doubt have had friends to assist you with certain skills. Maybe you trade labor with someone; i.e., you give him advice on tax preparation(using your logical-mathematical intelligence - remember Gardner's seven intelligences) and he helps you design a deck for his house(using your spatial intelligence). Today we may want to share the pleasures of a Caribbean Cruise with a traveling companion(a far cry from a covered wagon - how much pleasure was this bumpy ride!) There are many other pleasures or tasks for which friendship is needed. However, once these experiences are over, so is the relationship.

The third type is the "perfect friendship . . . of men who are good, and alike in **virtue**[Aristotle's highest good]; for these wish well alike to each other qua good, and they are good in themselves . . . therefore their friendship lasts as long as they are good - and goodness is an enduring thing. " **126** Aristotle is assuming the virtuous person will remain so. However, he doesn't explain from where goodness comes. The Apostle Paul sees goodness as one of the "fruits of the Holy Spirit", acquired as a result of asking another person of the Trinity(Jesus Christ) into our lives. **127**

Aristotle sees true friendship as characterized by the sharing of similar interests and tastes. . . .

"they wish to occupy themselves with their friends; and so some drink together, others dice together[possibly playing games or gambling] , others join in athletic exercises and hunting, or the study of philosophy, each . . . spending their days together in whatever they love most in life; for since they wish to live with their friends, they do and share in those things which give them the sense of living together." **128**

The above paragraph raises the interesting question, "According to Artistotle, can marriage partners also be the best of friends?" Yes, if they share commonalities such as travel, hobbies and similar standards of living. No, If they married according to the principle of attracting opposites. Aristotle's examples seem to apply to interests common to men. He could have also included interests common to women(remember he was writing over 2,000 years ago). Aristotle seems to imply it may be easier to share similar interests with friends. However, if your spouse is also your best friend, so much the better.

Finally, Aristotle deals with the issue of how many friends one needs. Although one may have many friends for specific purposes, true friendship is seen in another light. We may have many friends for utility, but the more favors they do for us, the more time it will take to return these favors. Aristotle cautions against having too many friends for pleasure. These friends evidently would not be virtuous! True friendship is selective: "One cannot be a friend to many people in the sense of having friendship of the perfect type with them, just as one cannot be in love with many people at once. . . Therefore friends in excess of those who are sufficient for our own life are superfluous. " **129** Even though Aristotle doesn't give us an exact number of friends we need, he sees a range of between too few and too many as the ideal. This is his concept of the "golden mean", which balances excess and defect(too little) to achieve a proper balance.

How many true friends - other than family members - do you have in one location. You can probably count them on one hand. If you have moved several times, you still have friends from your former residences. You may initially rely on them for socializing as you become acquainted in your new setting. Therefore you may possess a greater number of true friends from your former places of residence vis-a-vis your new location.

One of my fondest memories of living in Nebraska was the friends my wife and I developed. On Friday nights we used to "get together" with another couple at our respective houses. With classical music in the background and a little wine to drink, we would unwind from the week and began to share with each other. A warm fire on a cold winter night would provide an atmosphere for reflection. Sometimes we discussed raising our similarly - aged children. Other times we took on politics and religion - our favorite subjects you supposedly don't mix. So much for this taboo! We also discussed our travels and dreams for the future. In any case we engaged in a meaningful conversation. It was a friendly discussion as stimulating as that described by Solomon in Proverbs("as the sparks that fly when iron strikes iron.") **130**

Cooperation Among The Indians and the Emigrants

An account of travel along the Oregon Trail would not be complete without mentioning the role of Indians. Many stories and movies portray Indians as bloodthirsty savages looking for white scalps at every turn of the Trail. Look up at the bluff and there they are - dressed in their war paint, feathers and bonnets! See the emigrants circling the wagons to protect themselves from these impending raiders. As the Indians attack head-on the pioneers keep shooting until the "good guys" prevail.

How much of the above scenes are true? A more accurate portrayal is of Indians as beggars rather than attackers. Generally they "wanted only to talk and beg for handouts of sugar, tobacco and old clothes." **131** The most serious threat by Indians was not murder but horse thievery - a skill they demonstrated along the entire Trail(which of Gardner's intelligences would this be?) Unruh provides an example of this art form. An 1845 emigrant awoke one morning beyond South Pass to find his horse gone. He had tied the horse's rope around his arm before retiring for the night - to no avail! **132**

However, there were cases of murder of pioneers by Indians, especially west of South Pass. Travelers had to be ever watchful of this possibility. Most of these killings took place after the Trail became more crowded during the Gold Rush days of 1849 and beyond. Unruh compares the number of whites killed by Indians, and vice versa. From 1840-1848 Indians killed 34 whites while whites killed 26 Indians. During these first five years no whites were killed, along with only one Indian. Only four percent of all Trail deaths were due to Indian attacks - a far lower figure than commonly portrayed. In fact many instances of robbery and murder generally attributed to Indians were committed by whites disguised as Indians("white Indians"). **133**

A more common picture of white-Indian interaction would be one of cooperation and trade. Indians were hired to pilot emigrant wagons, stocks, belongings and even their families across treacherous rivers. Many took the advice of J.M. Shively who in 1846 recommended "you must hire an Indian to pilot you at the crossings of Snake River, it being dangerous if not perfectly understood." **134**

Other acts of cooperation involved pioneers hiring Indians traveling east to transport letters to their friends and relatives back home. Indians also performed occasional acts of kindness, such as pulling wagons up steep banks. They shared their knowledge of flora by advising which plants were edible. After Fort Boise the Indians traded for fresh salmon and vegetables. After months of eating a monotonous diet, this variety of healthful foods was greatly appreciated. **135**

Most of the interaction consisted of trading. The prized trading object for the whites were the Indian horses. Even though the Indians were shrewd bargainers, the white man's whiskey was usually sufficient to obtain these animals. Other bartered items included Indian moccasins, buffalo robes, lariats and ropes. In return the emigrants would give blankets and clothing to the Indians. **136**

In summary, a more accurate portrayal of white-Indian interaction should focus on aid and trade instead of hostilities. "Yet in spite of the frequent scares and thefts, almost everyone did complete the trip safely. . . " **137** Thus the Indians should be seen as making positive contributions to the pioneers, even though the latter crossed the former's lands.

Perceiving Indians Today

What's happened to the Indians since they roamed the plains during the frontier days? As the pioneers continued westward, more hostilities flared between whites and Indians. This resulted in several Indian Wars involving the U.S. Calvary. Victory usually belonged to the superior weaponry of the latter troops. With the Indians subdued and the frontier closed around 1890, a reservation system was established in the Western lands. Many Indians still live in these squalid conditions, marked by poverty, alcoholism and unemployment. In spite of government assistance programs, the Indians may be more of a problem for society today than they were to the pioneers 150 years ago - an interesting paradox. Government programs need to place more emphasis upon independence and self-reliance, rather than dependency and welfare.

However, some of the stereotypes are changing today. Indians are taking more pride in their identity, native customs and culture. Such groups as the American Indian Movement(AIM) are lobbying to aid Native Americans both on the reservations and in society at large. Movies such as "Dances With Wolves"(an Academy Award winner) illustrate a revisionist's view of this period of history. The positive aspects of the Indian culture, along with provocative acts by the whites, were more accurately portrayed. Hopefully, with more information of this type, the American Indians will finally achieve their rightful place in history and in today's society.

Lessons For Today

This lesson covered a wide range of interactions among the emigrants, between the emigrants and Indians - all with applicability for today's society. What can we learn from the pioneers' dependence on each other? **First**, a division of **responsibility** is an effective method to work together to accomplish specific tasks at home, school, church, job or in the community. **Second**, your **talents** will be more effectively utilized if they are matched with your skills and abilities. **Third**, you can build relationships with your spouse, family members, friends and neighbors by planning to spend more of your time in Covey's **Quadrant II** matrix. **Fourth**, critically evaluating portrayals of the **American Indian** in the media will result in more accurate images of them today and in history.

The next lesson will focus on two aspects necessary to a successful completion of the emigrant's journey: the disciplines needed and the obstacles they overcame. Stay on the Trail as we near the finish line!

"Interpretive Center, Baker, OR"

PRACTICING DISCIPLINE AND OVERCOMING OBSTACLES:

PRODUCING CHARACTER

170 days on the Oregon Trail! Plenty of time to encounter every possible obstacle - friction between individuals, thefts, accidents, disease, death, storms, hot and cold temperatures, unfriendly Indians, physical exhaustion of people and animals and lack of supplies. In spite of the above problems, most of the long days were the same. Monotony and discouragement were major concerns. In spite of these barriers, over 90% of those emigrants beginning in Independence made it to Oregon City. The pioneer spirit prevailed!

Today you hear many references to this pioneer spirit. Religious speakers use characters from the Bible as examples of this characteristic. Political leaders call upon us to sacrifice like the pioneers to accomplish a national goal. The assumption is we as Americans know what this type of spirit is, and believe it to be a positive trait to possess.

This lesson will focus on the following two aspects

of this pioneer spirit: (1) the importance of practicing discipline and (2) overcoming obstacles. These two ingredients produced the character needed to successfully achieve their "good life" in Oregon. Through understanding what the pioneers endured, we may be able to identify if we have this same pioneer spirit today.

The Pioneer Spirit: Practicing Discipline

Webster provides the following definitions for **discipline**:

1. Training that corrects, molds, or perfects the mental faculties or moral character

2. Orderly or prescribed conduct or pattern of behavior

3. Self-control **138**

Definition one relates to an individual habit producing character. The second definition relates to an organized collective society. The attribute enabling the above two definitions to become a reality is the third definition - self-control. The pioneers needed to implement all three definitions to successfully complete their journey.

In lesson eight a general picture was given of the various duties performed by the men, women and children. These tasks gave the journey a predictable order and pattern of conduct(definition two). These disciplines caused the journey to be more efficient, since new directions didn't have to be given at each campsite. It also eliminated confusion in determining who would perform a specific duty.

One of the best narratives of the daily routine on the Trail was written by Jesse Applegate. As you read his "A Day with the Cow Column of 1843," think of the disciplines involved in executing the duties described.

"It is four o'clock A.M.; the sentinels on duty have

discharged their rifles - the signal that the hours of sleep are over - and every wagon and tent is pouring forth its night tenants, and slow-kindling smokes begin largely to rise and float away in the morning air. Sixty men start from the corral, spreading as they make through the vast herd of cattle and horses that make a semicircle around the encampment, the most distant perhaps two miles away.

The herders pass to the extreme verge and carefully examine for trails beyond   to see that none of the animals have strayed or been stolen during the night. This morning no trails led beyond the outside animals in sight, and by 5 o'clock the herders begin to contract the great, moving circle, and the well-trained animals move slowly towards camp, clipping here and there a thistle or a tempting bunch of grass on the way. In about an hour five thousand animals are close up to the encampment, and the teamsters are busy selecting their teams and driving them inside the corral to be yoked.

. . . From 6 to 7 o'clock is a busy time; breakfast is to be eaten, the tents struck, the wagons loaded and the teams yoked and brought up in readiness to be attached to their respective wagons. All know when, at 7 o'clock, the signal to march sounds, that those not ready to take their proper places in the line of march must fall into the dusty rear for the day.

There are sixty wagons. They have been divided into fifteen divisions of platoons of four wagons each, and each platoon is entitled to lead in its turn. The leading platoon today will be the rear one tomorrow, and has lost his place in line, and is condemned to that uncomfortable post. It is within ten minutes of seven . . . the teams being attached to the wagons. The women and children have taken their places in them. The pilot . . . stands ready, in the midst of his pioneers and aides, to mount and lead the way. Ten or fifteen young men, not today on duty, form another cluster. They are ready to start on a buffalo hunt, are well mounted and well armed, as they need be, for the unfriendly Sioux have driven the buffalo out of the Platte, and the hunters must ride fifteen or twenty miles to reach them. The cow drivers are hastening, as they get ready, to the rear of their charge, to collect and prepare them for the day's march.

It is on the stroke of seven; the rush to and fro, the cracking of whips, the loud command to oxen, and what seemed to be the inextricable confusion of the last ten minutes has ceased. Fortunately, every one has been found and every teamster is at his post. The clear notes of a trumpet sound in the front; the pilot and his guards mount their horses; the leading divisions of the wagons move out of the encampment, and take up the line of march; the rest fall into their places with the precision of clock work. . ." **139**

Once the wagon train starts, the only break is for the noon meal. Once the guide selects the campsite for the night, a corral is formed for the animals by placing the wagons in a circle. Inside fires are lit and supper is cooked and eaten.

After supper a more relaxed atmosphere prevails. Applegate continues:

"It is not yet 8 o'clock when the first watch is to be set . . . Before a tent near the river a violin makes lovely music, and some youths and maidens have improvised a dance upon the green; in another quarter a flute gives its mellow and melancholy notes to the still night air, which, as they float away over the quiet river, seem a lament for past rather than a hope for the future. It has been a prosperous day; more than twenty miles have been accomplished of the great journey. Th encampment is a good one . . .

But time passes; the watch is set for the night; the council of old men has been broken up, and each has returned to his own quarter; the flute has whispered its last lament to the deepening night; the violin is silent, and the dancers have dispersed; enamored youth have whispered a tender "good night" in the ear of blushing maidens, or stolen a kiss from the lips of some future bride . . . All is hushed and reposed from the fatigues of the day, save the vigilant guard and the wakeful leader . . . He hears the 10 o'clock relief taking post and the "all well" report of the returned guard; the night deepens, yet he seeks not the needed repose . . . the last care of the day being removed, and the last duty performed, he too seeks the rest that will enable him to go through the same routine tomorrow." **140**

The various disciplines described by Applegate would be for the purpose of ensuring orderly conduct during the journey. Each person from the pilot to the children had specific tasks during the day. At night the role of the guards became important. The rest of the emigrants engaged in more relaxing and aesthetic activities. A balance seemed to exist between a disciplined and informal use of time during the 24 hour day. What disciplines are important for us to live a meaningful life today?

Practicing Peck's Disciplines

Discipline is just as important for us today as it was for the pioneers, with one exception. Even though we are not on a rigorous journey that requires discipline for survival, we need discipline to become self-actualized(more on this topic in the next lesson). The difference lies in the **voluntary** aspect of discipline today. Even though the emigrants chose to be part of the largest voluntary mass migration in the history of the United States, once on the Trail, discipline was a necessity. As adults today we can generally choose to exercise discipline in our free time. Usually no one tells us to read a good book instead of watching television, or jog instead of sitting in front of the TV. However, this aspect of free will makes the discipline of discipline more important. Sounds like a paradox.

Scott Peck opens his best-selling **The Road Less Traveled** by stating: "Life is difficult." **141** James asks his brothers in the Bible, "Is your life full of difficulties. . . ?" **142** Buddha taught that life was suffering. **143** The pioneers knew this truth and expected hardships along the way. So should we. How can we deal with problems along our "journey"?

Peck sees discipline as the method of solving our problems. It is not removing these obstacles, but meeting and overcoming them that gives meaning to life. Peck describes four techniques of suffering, or disciplines, needed to confront our problems: delayed gratification, acceptance of responsibility, dedication to reality and balancing.

Delayed Gratification

"Delayed gratification is the discipline of scheduling the pain and pleasures of life in such a way as to enhance the pleasure by meeting and experiencing the pain first and getting it over with." **144** The emigrants had to first endure the pain along the Trail to experience the pleasure of the "good life" in Oregon.

How difficult is this discipline to practice in today's society? Adages such as "just do it" and "buy now, pay later" are prevalent today. These images handsomely portrayed by the media portray a society consumed by instant gratification. You can have it all now! Hurry, this sale won't last long! Don't worry about the payments or consequences of smoking, excessive drinking(alcoholism) or sex with multiple partners(AIDS). Enjoy the moment! Television sitcoms solve all the problems in 30 minutes or less(less because of all the advertising!) This mindset sounds like the Biblical metaphor of the wide path leading to destruction. **145**

How can we practice delayed gratification today? We can counter the hedonistic advertising by "saving first, buying later." A good place to start is only to have one credit card, and use it only for guaranteeing lodging or car rental reservations. The pain of saving can enhance the pleasure of purchasing something you have needed or wanted for some time. You will also achieve satisfaction during the saving process. I have determined to only borrow money for appreciating items such as a house. This means I will save money for a car before its purchase. Because of delayed gratification, I'll probably always experience the pleasure of driving a debt-free used car. I have no expectations of ever owning a new car that depreciates after you drive it from the lot.

Encouraging your children to attend college before securing a job based on your talents(remember Gardner's seven intelligences) is another example of delayed gratification. Young people need to realize the training they are receiving now will literally pay in increased earning power later. According to a recent study, each additional year of college meant a wage increase of 16% when this person entered the job market. **146** Therefore the average college graduate will make 64% more in salary than a high school graduate.

A good test of deferred gratification is seen if your daughter or son aspires to become a physician. While still in medical school, their friends who have finished undergraduate school probably have landed good jobs and are driving new cars. You only have three - six years of school left! Hopefully your child will enjoy the process of acquiring an education, as well as the product of a satisfying and financially rewarding career. Then the pain can be turned into pleasure during the journey - not only at its destination.

Young couples dating can also delay the sex act until marriage. Married couples can enjoy each other - and only the other. The Sixth Commandment prohibiting adultery and admonitions against fornication take on new relevance in light of the AIDS epidemic. What we sow is what we reap. **147** Is God trying to tell us something about the pain of instant gratification?

Peck seems to think that instant gratification is associated with pain and delayed gratification with pleasure. However, I believe the former can also be pleasant if we enjoy the process. Remember "to smell the flowers along the way." With discipline and the help of Christ's power, we will be able to journey on the narrow road less traveled.

Acceptance Of Responsibility

Another tool for solving problems is to accept responsibility for them. We must decide which problems are within our jurisdiction to tackle. Covey uses two concentric circles to distinguish between our Circle of Concern and Circle of Influence(see Diagram 7). While we may be concerned with many topics(international tensions, environment, education, our work, our families), we may not be able to impact all these areas. He recommends a proactive posture by concentrating on those things you can influence(smaller circle). Another metaphor is to use the rifle rather than the shotgun approach to solving problems.

No Concern

Diagram 7

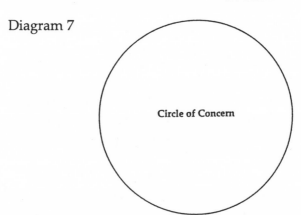

Circle of Concern

From Covey, The Seven Habits of Highly Effective People, 1989,81.

The emigrants organized their wagon trains by assigning tasks to individuals. For example, if the women didn't cook, a basic need would not be satisfied. If the men didn't hitch the oxen to the wagons each morning, the "train" wouldn't move. Even the children's failure to collect wood or buffalo chips would mean a cold meal. Failure to exercise these responsibilities would mean adverse consequences for the entire wagon train.

Once we have accepted responsibility to solve our problems, we have choices as to possible courses of action.

You may hear an individual say something like, "I had no choice but to divorce my spouse." But we always have choices. The teacher in one of my church classes put it succinctly, "Life is choices." **148**

We have choices in our attitudes, thoughts, words and actions. We can take either a mainly optimistic or pessimistic view of our circumstances. Is your "glass of life" half full or half empty? Is the sky partly sunny or partly cloudy? Can you make lemonade from lemons?

If anybody had reason to be pessimistic, it was Viktor Frankel. A prominent Austrian Jewish psychiatrist, Frankel's career was disrupted when the Nazis threw him into a concentration camp during World War II. He saw many of his fellow prisoners die as they were deprived of Maslow's basic needs. He was deprived of privacy, dignity and freedom of movement. Through this ordeal Frankel realized there was one thing the guards could not take away from him. In **Man's Search For Meaning**, Frankel states it this way: ". . . everything can be taken from a man but one thing: the last of the human freedoms - to **choose** one's attitude in any given set of circumstances, to choose one's own way." **149** Choosing a positive attitude in the midst of adversity requires a discipline leading to high moral character(remember our first definition of discipline).

Another example of choosing a positive attitude toward enemies was shown by Christ on the cross. In the midst of His suffering, he could still plead for his Father "to forgive them, for they don't know what they are doing." **150** Since our attitudes affect our thoughts, words and actions, this discipline is very important today. Choosing a positive attitude along the Trail was a challenge for the pioneers. It still is for us on our modern "journey."

Dedication To Reality

Pontius Pilate asked Jesus the provocative question, "What is truth?" **151** Jesus claimed to be the truth that would set us free. **152** Webster defines truth as "the body of real things, events and facts." **153** Peck agrees with Webster when he sees truth as reality.

The only trouble is that people have different perceptions of reality. Covey states: ". . . people see the world, not as it is, but as they are." **154** We react to our perceptions of reality(Peck calls them our maps), even though this perception is inaccurate, or our maps are outdated. For example, if we think someone doesn't like us, we will probably respond negatively - unless we develop Frankel's attitude. Maybe that person does like us in reality, but instead we respond to our perception of that person's perception of us. These human interactions can become complicated! That's why we need psychiatrists. That's why we need to constantly ask Pilate's question, and challenge our perceptions of reality.

The pioneers needed an accurate map of reality - literally - to complete their "good life journey." Before starting they no doubt weighed the **costs** of traveling the Trail with the **benefits** of reaching their destination. The costs would involve such emotional hardships as leaving their friends and families, and experiencing loneliness on the Trail. Physical costs could include fatigue, sickness and possibly death. The economic benefits would be the chance to successfully raise crops and livestock on the fertile farmland in Oregon. The spirit of adventure and their willingness to take the risk to travel would be intrinsic benefits. This discipline of dedication to reality was essential for the pioneers to reach their goal.

Peck postulates three methods of dedicating ourselves to reality. **First** is continuous self-examination. Socrates' statement, "The unexamined life is not worth living," is relevant here. Aristotle amplifies this statement by concluding the contemplative life is the best type of living. Peck sees wisdom as contemplation plus action. **155**

Second, striving to live the truth means a willingness to be challenged. We must be able to accept criticism - not all of it constructive - from our spouses, children, work associates and friends. We should care more about **what** is right than **who** is right - even if the who is not ourself. This is principled living.

We must be open to changing our perception of reality. This is where discipline comes into play. The easiest thing would be to refuse to listen to others, and maintain our view of reality. However, this may not lead us to the truth. We surely won't grow toward Maslow's self-actualization in this manner. A healthy self-concept(remember this discussion in the first lesson) will allow us to be open to others' suggestions.

Third, a life of total dedication to the truth means total honesty. This starts with being true to ourselves. We need to search our attitudes, thoughts, and motives to see if they are congruent with our actions toward others. The Quaker desire that the inward and outward man(or woman) become one certainly applies here. Our walk should match our talk.

However, most people are not completely honest(hypocritical is the common accusation in this case) with others or themselves. They take the popular easy road, not the one less traveled. "Yet the rewards of the difficult life of honesty and dedication to the truth are more than commensurate with the demands. By virtue of the fact that their maps are continually being challenged, open people are continually growing people." **156**

Balancing

Peck calls balancing the "discipline required to discipline discipline." **157** This type of discipline gives us the **flexibility** to respond to a particular situation based on the information at the time. Even though we adhere to certain principles, they do not become rigid dogmas preventing us from considering alternatives.

One example of flexibility comes from the world of politics. In 1992 President Clinton campaigned for a middle class tax cut as a means of stimulating the stagnant economy. Ironically, after the election, favorable economic reports indicated an end to the recession. With this new information Mr. Clinton stated there may not be a need for this tax reduction. He is demonstrating balancing by this policy change("The American people would think I was foolish if I said I would not respond to changing circumstances." **158**) Critics say he broke his campaign promise - another typical politician. What's a voter to believe?

Aristotle's "Golden Mean"

The idea of achieving a balance between extremes was articulated in Aristotle's **Nicomachean Ethics.** This discipline was the habit of making "right" choices. A person possessing the character of moral virtue would consistently choose a course of action between two vices, the one involving excess, the other deficiency. This intermediate path has been called the "golden mean" and could be depicted on the following continuum:

Deficiency   Virtue("golden mean")   Excess

Aristotle concludes, " . . . the intermediate state is in all things to be praised, but that we must incline sometimes towards the excess, sometimes towards the deficiency; for so shall we most easily hit the mean and what is right." **159**

Aristotle provides many relevant examples of how the path of moderation can lead to excellence. In regards to spending money, the following continuum would apply where liberality is the "golden mean" between the deficiency of stinginess and the excess of extravagance:

Spending Money

Extravagance   Liberality   Stinginess

154

With the emotion of anger, the mean state of gentleness is buffered between the extremes of impassivity and passionateness as depicted below:

Anger

_____

| Impassivity | Gentleness | Passionateness |

You may use the continuum below to name a discipline or character trait you would like to cultivate, together with its deficiency and excess. Your goal is to experience the "golden mean" in this aspect of your life. Best wishes as you strive toward excellence!

Character Trait:

_____

| Deficiency: | Mean: | Excess: |

Balancing The Four Dimensions Of Our Nature

Each person is composed of the following four dimensions:

The physical - our bodies
The spiritual - our center
The mental - our mind
The social - our relationships with others

A balanced life would be spending time in each of these four areas. The amount of time we spend in each area does not have to be equal, but each area should be represented daily. Covey's 7th Habit of "Sharpening The Saw" involves spending a minimum of one hour daily in renewing the physical, spiritual and mental dimensions of our lives. This Daily Private Victory provides the intrinsic foundation to effectively relate to others in the social area - thus giving you Daily Public Victory as well. **160** Covey provides examples of how we can cultivate each area of our life(see Diagram 8) to achieve a balanced and meaningful life.

Diagram 8

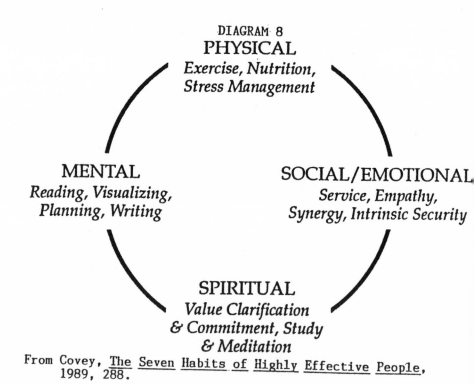

DIAGRAM 8

PHYSICAL
Exercise, Nutrition,
Stress Management

MENTAL
Reading, Visualizing,
Planning, Writing

SOCIAL/EMOTIONAL
Service, Empathy,
Synergy, Intrinsic Security

SPIRITUAL
Value Clarification
& Commitment, Study
& Meditation

From Covey, The Seven Habits of Highly Effective People, 1989, 288.

Examples Of The Balanced Life

Throughout history certain individuals exhibited the discipline of living a balanced life. The Bible portrays the four dimensions of **Jesus'** life. He grew tall(physically) and wise(mentally), being loved by God(spiritually) and man(socially). **161** Even though He had a public ministry to the needy(social), Jesus spent much time alone praying to His father(spiritual). He was learned in the Scriptures and no doubt well versed in the great literature of His day(mental). Walking from town to town during His ministry kept His body in good condition(physical). By being attuned to His four natures, Jesus was able to accomplish His mission on earth. Today His influence extends throughout the world.

During our family's visit to Monticello, **Thomas Jefferson's** home, we learned about the balanced life of our third president. He was always up at sunrise, ready to maximize his day. We were told the sun never shone on Jefferson in bed (his bed was placed to receive the first rays of dawn). Throughout his entire life, he always arose with the sun - an amazing discipline! The morning hours were occupied with his writings. His main ideas were conveyed through over 1,000 letters to his friends(mental). The afternoons were devoted to riding his horse around Monticello's well-kept grounds, where he supervised its care(physical). Mr. Jefferson kept the evenings to gather with family and friends(social). **The Jefferson Bible**, his synthesis of the life of Jesus from the Gospels, demonstrated Jefferson's spiritual interest. Because of Thomas Jefferson's many contributions to democracy and his disciplined life, one columnist nominated him for "Man of the Millennium."

The **Pioneers** attempted a balanced life along the Trail. Their main concerns were at Maslow's physiological and safety levels(physical). This arduous journey required physical stamina to reach Oregon City. Many of them walked the entire 2,000 miles! It was more comfortable than riding in the bumpy covered wagons. Still they took time at night to relax with their family and friends, singing and telling stories around the campfire(social). Some of them recorded their experiences in journals(mental). Sunday was usually a day for church services and rest(spiritual).

Christ, Jefferson and the Pioneers are three models of the disciplined, balanced life. How can we allocate our time among the spiritual, physical, mental and social components of our daily lives? What is your plan?

I usually start the day by reading from the Bible(spiritual). Walking, biking or cross-country skiing permit me the needed solitude to think, pray and exercise(physical). Reading a self-improvement book(like Covey's) challenges me mentally. Engaging friends in a meaningful discussion, or communicating with my family can be enjoyable activities(social).

Overcoming Obstacles

Character = discipline + overcoming obstacles. Whereas discipline must be practiced, obstacles must be overcome. Certainly the pioneers had many obstacles. So do we. The test is how we handle these barriers. Do we succumb or overcome?

Pioneer Obstacles

The emigrants - to reach the "good life" in Oregon - needed to conquer two types of obstacles. The first were causes leading to the **deaths** of some of their traveling companions. The second were the **hardships** the survivors needed to conquer.

Causes Of Death

Would you start on a journey today knowing you would have approximately a **one in ten** chance of dying enroute? That's what the pioneers who started for their "good life" faced. Estimates of deaths on the Oregon-California Trail range from a low of 12,000 to a high of 30,000, with an average of approximately 20,000. **162** Their travel was considerably more risky than traveling today's interstate highways.

The leading cause of death on the Trail was **disease** - accounting for 9 of every 10 deaths. **163** The most severe disease was the dreaded cholera. "This acute infection results from the consumption of water or foods contaminated by human wastes infected with the cholera bacterium. Vomiting and severe diarrhea are the major symptoms . . . and can result in dehydration, hypovolemic shock and death." **164** It struck so quickly that someone with cholera in the morning may have died that evening. The frequency of this disease was highest east of Fort Laramie. "By the time the emigrants reached Fort Laramie about ninety-one percent of the cholera deaths were behind them and by South Pass, ninety-six percent." **165**

Two other serious diseases were "mountain fever" and scurvy. The former was contracted in the higher elevations beyond Fort Laramie. Today this malady is known as Rocky Mountain Fever or Colorado tick fever. Because of months without sufficient fresh fruit and vegetables, many emigrants succumbed to the latter disease during the last leg of the arduous journey. The Indians were a Godsend by furnishing these precious foods when needed most. Even though deaths from these diseases were rare, the hardships were widespread. **166**

The second most common type of death along the Trail was due to **accidents**. **Drownings** were the most frequent mishap, with many fatalities recorded in the Platte River(even though today it is "a mile wide and a foot deep") and the Green River crossing. Most diaries record a drowning or the "near misses" they witnessed. For example, in one twenty-four period in 1847 two women were widowed and nine children were left fatherless at the Snake River crossing. **167** Nearly two-thirds of the drownings occurred west of South Pass and before 1854 - when bridges and ferries were not as common. **168**

The second most common type of accident was **care-lessness** in using firearms. Most emigrants, fearing the unknown and hostile Indians, carried a veritable arsenal in their wagons. William Kelly described their twenty-five man company as marching off to war:" ... but we were well equipped, each man carrying in his belt a revolver, a sword, and bowie-knife; the mounted men having besides a pair of holster-pistols and a rifle slung from the horn of their saddles, over and above which there were several double and single-shot guns and rifles suspended in the wagons, in loops, near the forepart, where they would be easily accessible in case of attack." **169** It was no wonder that some of these weapons would discharge. Many of these deaths resulted when an emigrant removed his gun from their wagon-muzzle first! Not surprisingly, nine-tenths of these mishaps occurred east of South Pass - when they were still getting used to traveling with their weapons. "Several overlanders acknowledged that they were much more frightened of carelessly handled guns in their own trains than they were of any hostile Indians." **170**

Other accidents resulted from wagon mishaps, usually involving animals. Adults and children fell from wagons and under their wheels. Such was the case of Joel Hembree's six-year old son Joel who in 1843, "... fell off the wagon tung & both wheels run over him." **171**

Deaths due to Indian attacks have been overplayed. As mentioned in the previous lesson, most Indians were friendly and assisted the emigrants. Unruh estimates only four percent of trail deaths were caused by Indians. From 1843-1848 (before the California Gold Rush), only 34 whites were killed by Indians. Most of these deaths were West of South Pass. **172**

As the above examples illustrate, death along the entire Trail was a serious consideration. A higher percentage of death from disease and firearms occurred east of South Pass. West of this halfway point the dangers were more from drownings and Indian attack. Estimates of death along the Trail vary from (1) one for every twenty five feet (2) one per five hundred feet or (3) seventeen per mile. 173 In any case the "Grim Reaper" was always stalking the emigrants. Sometimes he caught up with them!

Hardships

The 2,000 mile journey to Oregon was a marathon, not a sprint. Therefore the pioneers needed to pace themselves and their animals so they would be able to cross the finish line at Oregon City. Instead of "hitting the wall" as the long distance runners do, the emigrants "saw the elephant." This latter expression personified total exhaustion on the Trail - a phenomenon faced by many weary emigrants. Still most kept going.

The obstacles faced by the pioneers were **natural** and **man-made.** The former hardships related to the changing **weather** conditions(see lesson seven). These travelers needed to be ready for sudden prairie storms, complete with their own sound and light shows. Stifling dust storms were more common the farther west they traversed this arid climate. This climate caused the wooden wheels to shrink and suddenly fall off the covered wagons. The searing summer heat was replaced by the cold nights, especially at the higher altitudes of the western plateaus. In the mountains, snow and blizzards replaced rain as the precipitation to avoid .

They couldn't escape the adverse elements as we usually can today. No air-conditioned wagons. No houses with basements to protect them from the storms. No electronic air filters to keep the dust down. No furnace to keep them warm at night. No rubber tires only needing more air to stay on your automobile axles.

When weather was threatening, they simply "battened down the hatches" and rode out the storms. When "the sun came out tomorrow" they continued their trek - one day at a time.

Even though the men, women and children exhibited discipline in attending to the daily duties, much **hard**

work was involved. Six months of cooking the same food over a fire, rounding up livestock and gathering firewood could become drudgery. Without the modern conveniences we take for granted(stoves, microwaves, refrigerators, dishwashers and even trash compactors), preparing meals and cleaning up afterwards took hours per day. They didn't even have noisy chainsaws to chop their sparse firewood. No automatic buffalo chip gatherer either - they did this by hand! No pickups to round up the livestock. Attending to these basic Maslowian needs took longer than the equivalent chores today. This is probably why relaxing, singing and socializing at night was so important to provide for the higher level needs of these pioneers.

Another physical hardship was the **exhaustion** of the people and animals along the way. The lack of fresh fruit for the emigrants and adequate food for the animals contributed to this problem. Since many persons walked the entire 2,000 miles, fatigue could be a factor. How many of us walk 500 miles per month?

Women seemed to bear the brunt of the hardships on the journey. Maybe they did most of the work. Maybe they lacked the stamina of the men. In any case most of them exhibited determination in completing their tasks as illustrated by the following description near the Kansas River crossing in 1844:

" . . . and here let me say there was one young Lady which showed herself
worthy of the bravest undaunted pioneer of (the) west for after having
kneaded her dough she watched and nursed the fire and held an umbrella
over the fire and her skillit with the greatest composure for near 2 hours and
baked bread enough to give us a very plentifull supper. . . " **174**

As the emigrants' shoes wore out, so did their livestock. Many animals simply gave out and died in their tracks.

They succumbed to pulling heavy wagons. Even though the emigrants jettisoned their weighty possessions, it may have not been enough to save their oxen. Other causes of live-stock deaths were insufficient grass and water(two of the basics of the trip). Many died of starvation or thirst. Because of the metal collars, animals were a target for lightning during the violent thunderstorms on the plains. There was an inverse relationship between human and animal deaths. Most emigrant deaths occurred during the first half of the journey, whereas the majority of animal deaths happened during the last half, when exhaustion was more of a factor. **175**

Problems due to **criminals and thieves** constituted a hardship to the victims. Even though Indians stole pioneer horses, theft among the whites also occurred. Objects could include tools, food, firearms, firewood or jewelry. Whites dressed as Indians("white Indians") would commit these crimes, hoping to escape punishment through their disguises. Satisfying this need for safety 150 years ago may have been easier than many "civilized" areas of our country today. At least the pioneers had no stereos, televisions or VCRs to steal!

Psychological hardships related to **homesickness, loneliness** and **monotony.** Even though goodbyes were exchanged when the emigrants left their homes in the East and Midwest, the long journey afforded much time to think. Pioneers may have remembered the "conveniences" of home and the good times spent with family and friends. They couldn't "reach out and touch" their loved ones with a telephone call. Even if they wrote a letter, no Pony Express was available. They did use the "roadside telegraph" for "go backs" traveling east to civilization. Forget the fax machines and cellular phones. Even smoke signals wouldn't travel east of the Missouri!

Up at 4 in the morning. Break camp. Fix and eat breakfast at six. On the road by 7. Walk or ride until noon. Stop for lunch. Travel until the sun is low on the horizon. Set up camp. Prepare and eat dinner. Relax, sing or socialize until dark. Retire to bed until 4 the next morning. Do this approximately 180 times from May to November of 1843 enroute from Independence to Oregon City. Sounds monotonous. It was! The emigrants may have subconsciously welcomed the diversity provided by changing weather conditions, Indian encounters or diseases as a temporary escape from the daily grind - provided no deaths resulted from these hardships.

How did they cope with this routine? Some kept journals of their experiences. Others looked forward to the aesthetic beauty of the landmarks described in lesson six. The time at night was important for socializing with friends. All emigrants had much time to think and dream as they slowly lurched forward toward their "good life" goal in Oregon.

An anonymous overlander in 1852 summarized the hardships on the journey(notice the preoccupation with lower level needs):

> "To enjoy such a trip along with such a crowd of emigration, a man must be able to endure heat like a Salamander, mud and water like a muskrat, dust like a toad, and labor like a jackass. He must learn to eat with his unwashed fingers, drink out of the same vessel with his mules, sleep on the ground when it rains, and share his blanket with vermin, and have patience with musketoes, who don't know any difference between the face of a man and the face of a mule, but dash without ceremony from one into the other. He must cease to think, except as to where he may find grass and water and a good camping place. It is a hardship without glory, to be sick without a home, to die and be buried like a dog." **176**

Coping With Hardships Today

We all have hardships today. Remember Peck's opening quote for his book("Life is difficult.") Our obstacles may not be the same as those encountered by the pioneers. Middle and upper class Americans usually don't worry about pre-mature death and serious diseases. We are generally safe from criminals in our suburban homes and neighborhoods. Our houses protect us from adverse weather conditions. We can eat nutritious meals and exercise to avoid exhaustion. We can "reach out and touch" a distant friend or relative with our pushbutton phone, or pen and stationery.

However, we do experience hardships of a different kind. We have **financial** difficulties due to the loss of a job(this is happening today, especially among white-collar workers). Our parents or immediate family member may contract a serious **disease** such as cancer or heart trouble. Our **family** relationships may be changed by divorce or sepa-ration. We may experience **stress** because of hectic sched-ules in our fast-paced modern living.

How do we overcome these obstacles? Do we try to remove them and make the way smooth for us and our chil-dren? John Rosemond, a contemporary conservative psy-chologist, says no. Children need to learn how to work through their problems. So do adults. This is the way to develop character and "earn" positive self-esteem.

Cradles of Eminence details the study of four hun-dred Twentieth Century eminent persons. The husband and wife psychologist team of Victor and Mildred Goertzel con-cluded that even though there was a love of learning in most of these homes, "three-fourths of the children [were] troubled - by poverty; by a broken home; by rejecting, overposses-sive, estranged, or dominating parents; by financial ups and downs; by physical handicaps; or by parental dissatisfaction over the children's school failures or vocational choices. " 177 However, these barriers were overcome by these deter-mined men and women. Had these problems not been a part of their early lives, these outstanding persons may not have developed the character(discipline plus overcoming obstacles) essential to making contributions for our society.

The apostle James summarizes the findings of Rosemond and the Goertzels vis-a-vis character: "... is your life full of difficulties and temptations? Then be happy, for when the way is rough, your patience has a chance to grow. So let it grow, and don't try to squirm out of your problems. For when your patience is finally in full bloom, then you will be ready for anything, strong in character, full and complete." **178** Character building is a lifelong process. The pioneers experienced it on their journey. Hopefully we are also growing toward this goal in our lives.

The pioneers have now overcome the obstacles on their journey. Soon they will reach their "good life" in Oregon. Our last lesson deals with what they and we will learn by achieving goals. We're almost to our new home! Keep on the Trail!

"Display, Oregon City, OR"

ACHIEVING THE GOAL: ARRIVING IN OREGON CITY

One more state to go! When the pioneers came over Flagstaff Hill in arid Eastern Oregon, the landscape suddenly became more colorful. For the first time they saw the **green** trees on the **white**, snow-capped Blue Mountains. Add to this a bright, **yellow** sun against a cloudless **blue** sky, and you have the four colors mentioned in Lesson Seven. Remember colortherapy. It probably combatted pioneer depression.

But by November the 1843 Emigrants were experiencing the gray "Oregon Rain" as they slogged westward along the Columbia River, or rafted down this "River of the West." Many of their rafts capsized on this dangerous part of the journey. But they were ever so close to reaching their goal!

Finally on November 13, after battling all the hardships described in the previous lesson - this party of 875 hardy pioneers, lurching in approximately 120 wagons, reached their destination - Oregon City! That must have been an emotional moment for the weary emigrants! Time to hoist the flag or bring out the champagne! However, one emigrant simply records, "Reached Oregon City. Went to work the next day."

They had traveled **1932 miles** from their starting point in Independence, Missouri. They assembled on May 22 from Elm Grove, their take-off point 12 miles west of Independence. **179** This longest voluntary mass migration in human history took **176 days** and averaged **eleven miles per day**. No Indy 500 speed records broken here! But Winston Churchill would have been proud of their **task commitment**. Remember his famous challenge to the British people during the dark days of World War II, "Never, never, never give up!"

Evaluating The Journey

It's now time to travel above the dusty Trail and take a holistic view of this epic trip. We will discuss the following evaluative questions:

1. Which was more important, the journey or the destination?

2. Was this trip worth it for the pioneers?

3. Did the emigrants obtain the "good life?"

4. Were the overlanders satisfied once they reached Oregon?

All these questions are relevant to our "journey." Come along for a modern mental helicopter ride, blending the present with the past.

Is It The Journey Or The Destination?

It would have been interesting to be a "mouse in the wagon," observing the personalities of the emigrants 150 years ago. Some of the people would be enjoying this great adventure by "smelling the roses" along the way. They would take time to enjoy the aesthetic beauty(Maslow's highest level) of such landmarks as Chimney Rock and the Blue Mountains. Maybe they would even sketch these wonders of God's Handiwork. Making friends along the way was important for these "happy campers." They enjoyed sharing their daily traveling experiences - particularly minor incidents - around the campfire at night. These gregarious folks would be leading the fiddling and singing at night. They looked forward to this relaxing time. Whether they traveled 5 or 25 miles a day wasn't important to them. The enjoyment of the journey was more important.

Others had a more determined look as they faced the western horizon. They were probably leading the wagon trains and encouraging the others to speed up to reach their goal. These wagon masters would be constantly warning of possible early snows in the mountains, and the need to climb them before winter set in. Emigrants traveling after 1847 needed only to invoke the Donner Party as a horrifying reminder of what can happen when you "smell the flowers" too long. These leaders didn't take time to socialize during the day or around the campfire at night. They were too busy planning the fastest route to Oregon - where they would find their "good life."

With which of these groups do you identify? The first group of emigrants are more **relational-oriented.** For them the **journey** is more important than the destination. They take time to "smell the flowers." They would probably be predominantly "laid back Type B" personalities, subject to less stress and heart attacks. They would not worry about accomplishing goals - even if they established them. Their pioneer T-shirts would read: "Whatever will be, will be," "Don't worry, be happy" or "Type B's have more fun." This group is content to be at Maslow's belonging level, with little interest in becoming self-actualized.

The latter group is **achievement-oriented.** They are committed to the task at hand - getting to the Promised Land before the winter snows. Their flowers will be waiting for them at their **destination** - not along the Trail! These overlanders may exhibit an abrasive personality in their relations with others who do not share their high expectations. You can tell them by their "pioneer planners" - complete with route maps, daily mileage logs and campsites. However, these "Type A" achievers are subject to stress and heart attacks. For this driven group, reaching their goal in Oregon is evidence they have become self-actualized and have reached the "good life."

What about our journey through life? Do we prefer to take the fast "Type A" interstate highways enroute to our goal of success - hurrying to a better paying job with more prestige and status? Or do we enjoy the relaxing trip of the less traveled but slower "Type B blue highways" - taking time to develop relationships with our family and friends?

Ralph Waldo Emerson seems to blend achievement with relationships in his version of "Success:"

> "How do you measure success?
> To laugh often and much;
> To win the respect of intelligent people,
> And the affection of children.
> To earn the appreciation of honest critics,
> And to endure the betrayal of false friends.
> To appreciate beauty, to find the best in others,
> To leave the world a bit better . . .
> Whether by a healthy child, a garden patch,
> A redeemed social condition, or a job well done.
> To know even one life has breathed easier
> Because you have live.
> This is to have succeeded." **180**

May success of this type be our goal as we continue our "journey."

Was The Journey Worth It?

This question couldn't be answered as the overlanders trudged mile after monotonous mile over the Trail. They were too preoccupied with satisfying the lower level needs of Maslow's Hierarchy(Physiological and Safety). However, after their successful arrival in Oregon, they could begin to put this higher level question in perspective. During the process of becoming settlers, these pioneers had time to reflect on their journey. The longer they were in the Willamette Valley, the broader their perspective.

One way to answer this question is to analyze the pros and cons of the journey. This left-brain approach would look as follows:

Pros(Worth It?)	Cons(Not Worth It?)
1. **Economic** - good land producing abundant harvests, livestock game and trees for building; plentiful streams for fish	1. **Hardships** along the way (see Lesson Nine)
	2. **Hardships** in getting established in Oregon
2. **Health** - climate conducive for good health	3. **Separation** from friends and relatives back East
3. **Aesthetic** - able to enjoy natural beauty of mountains and oceans	4. **Loss** of friends and relatives who died on the Trail
4. **Invigorating** - opportunity to make a fresh start with new friends in a new location	5. **Lack of cultural opportunities** in Oregon
5. **Enhanced self-esteem** - from taking the risk to successfully complete the journey	

Undoubtedly, more pros and cons could be added to he above list. However, this gives you the idea that the "glass in Oregon" could be either half-full or half-empty. Since the vast majority of emigrants who reached Oregon stayed permanently, the preponderance of evidence favors the **pros** over the cons. Pioneer pride is still evident in today's Oregonians, who enjoy tracing their ancestry back to these emigrants.

When we are facing a big decision today - such as a move - we may use the above system of analyzing the pros and cons. This left-brain approach for me usually means writing the pros and cons on a yellow legal pad - on each side of a vertical line I draw down the middle. I may also assign numerical values to each argument, using a scale of 1-5 - with the most important points receiving the higher numbers. The decision to move(pro) or not to move(con) then can be made by simply totaling the numbers on each side. The side comprising the higher number is your decision.

However, the integrity of this system is compromised by working it backwards - you intuitively decide what you want to do, and then adjust the arguments and numbers to fit this outcome! This right-brain approach (without the numbers) is much quicker and may be as valid. In any case, you have two methods of making decisions. Depending upon your learning style, you will probably prefer one. Try it and see if it works for you.

Did The Pioneers Achieve The "Good Life?"

Throughout these lessons many references have been made to the "good life." The emigrants saw Oregon as the place where they could obtain this lofty goal. However, before you can achieve a goal you must not only visualize its attainment, but also define it.

What was the pioneers' perception of their "good life?" It was mainly seen in **economic** terms - a beautiful, bountiful land of "milk and honey" producing bumper crops. There were other less obvious elements of this ideal life. They included **good health, the spirit of adventure** in making new friends in a new environment, the **satisfaction** of accomplishing their goal, and an appreciation of the **natural beauty** surrounding their new homes in the Willamette Valley.

Today references are made to finding the "good life." One state uses it as its motto("Nebraska: The good life"). I saw this sign many times heading west across "the wide Missouri" from my native adjacent state of Iowa. Resort and vacation areas champion the "good life" in their advertisements. These references - never defined - are designed to create a positive mental picture of this type of lifestyle. As in the days of the pioneers, the predominant appeal is economic - a place where your basic needs are met and you can enjoy a safe, friendly and leisurely life.

Is this how Aristotle and Maslow depicted the "good life?" There is more to it than the ideas of both the emigrants and contemporary Americans. Lesson Two compares Aristotle's limited and unlimited real goods with Maslow's Hierarchy of Needs(refer to Diagrams 1 and 2). The former's real goods can be equated with the latter's lower level needs. Aristotle's unlimited real goods are equivalent to Maslow's higher levels. The "good life" is found at these highest levels of both hierarchies.

Maslow used the term **self-actualization** to describe a person who is living a fulfilled life and has reached her/his potential. In **Motivation and Personality,** Maslow succinctly describes self-actualization as, "What a person can be, he must be." **181** He sees the desire for self-fulfillment as becoming "more and more what one is, to become everything one is capable of becoming." **182** According to Maslow, only a person who has basically satisfied the four lower needs(physiological, safety, belongingness and esteem) can become self-actualized. The U.S. Army's recruiting slogan, "Be all that you can be . . . " seems related to this quest. Maslow's studies reveal that only a fraction of one percent of the adult population becomes self-actualized. Most of these "few good people" are over sixty years of age and are moving toward maturity. Maslow calls them "fully human."

More sophisticated definitions of self-actualization appear in a newer book by Maslow. In **Toward A Psychology of Being**, self-actualization is defined as:

1. Ongoing actualization of potentials, capacities and talents
2. Fulfillment of a mission(or call, fate, destiny, or vocation)
3. A fuller knowledge of, and acceptance of, the person's own intrinsic nature **184**

In reaching Oregon the pioneers fulfilled definition two above. The external conditions(fertile land and the opportunity for a fresh start) were conducive for them to use their abilities for economic success. Settling in Oregon was a strong reason the Oregon Territory became American instead of British. Remember the mission called "Manifest Destiny." Definitions one and three are more personal in nature. It relates to accepting yourself and your God-given gifts and talents. Perhaps some emigrants reached this level - but the diaries don't reveal this type of introspection.

How about you? Are you utilizing your abilities to the fullest? Do you have a clearly defined mission in life? Are you pursuing it? Have you accepted yourself as you are while trying to reach your potential? Maybe the following list will assist you in answering these reflective questions?

Maslow delineates the following characteristics of self-actualized people as(parentheses mine):

1. realistically oriented; objective; seeing life clearly

2. accepting themselves(positive self-concept), other people and the natural world for what they are; possessing a low degree of self conflict

3. having the courage to give up personal defense mechanisms

4. problem-centered rather than self-centered in the sense of being able to devote their attention to an important job, task, duty or mission that seems particularly cut out for them(task-commitment)

5. their work becomes play; their vocation and avocation are the same

6. having a need for privacy and even seeking it out on occasion, needing it for periods of intense concentration and total absorption on subjects of interest to them("passions")

7. autonomous, independent and able to remain true to themselves in the face of rejection and unpopularity

8. having a great capacity for creativity, as expressed by flexibility, spontaneity, courage, risk-taking and openness in thinking, emotions and behavior

9. having a continuous freshness of appreciation and capacity to stand in awe again and again of the basic goods of life(aesthetic)

10. having frequent "mystic" or "peak" experiences, although not necessarily religious in character; listening to these "inner voices"

11. feeling a sense of identification with mankind as a whole in the sense of being concerned not only with the lot of their own immediate families, but with the welfare of the world as a whole

12. having intimate relationships with only a few specifically loved people that tend to be profound and deeply emotional rather than superficial(friendships); enjoys people but doesn't depend upon them

13. needing less love from others, but able to give more love to others

14. having a highly developed sense of ethics and a clear notion of right and wrong

15. having an unhostile sense of humor, which is expressed in their capacity to make common human foibles, pretensions and foolishness the subject of laughter, rather than smut, sadism or hatred of authority

16. resisting total conformity to culture; daring to be different and making decisions in the face of unpopular opinions; governed more by inner desires than by society

17. making choices for growth instead of for defense, fear or safety

18. humility; having the ability to listen carefully to others

19. concerned more with ends than means **185**

It is important to remember "self-actualization is an ongoing process" and "is a matter of degree, of little accessions accumulated one by one." These people never arrive. They are always growing intellectually, spiritually, physically and socially. "Self-actualizing[not self-actualized] people enjoy life in general and in practically all its aspects, while most other people enjoy only stray moments of triumph, of achievement or of climax or peak experience. They never tire of life." **186**

Once the pioneers settled in Oregon and worked to make a comfortable life for their families, their basic needs(physiological and safety) were probably met - assuming the elements of Nature cooperated to provide abundant harvests. They established friends and neighbors who supported each other in good and bad times. These needs being basically satisfied would increase their sense of esteem and confidence in themselves. Even though these higher level needs were generally met, some of them may not have been content to live at these levels. They were striving to become self-actualized - even though they may not have realized it. Therefore some of the above characteristics may have been pursued by a small minority of settlers.

Assuming your basic needs are generally satisfied, how many of the above characteristics have you experienced? Can you provide examples of how these traits have been important in your life? If you can, you may be on the road to self-actualization - and you thought this "good life road" led to Oregon! It did for the pioneers.

Once a person has experienced many of the above self-actualization characteristics, other needs become become paramount for these rare individuals. Both Aristotle and Maslow address them(see Diagrams 1 and 2). What Maslow calls the search for **knowledge** Aristotle calls **goods of the mind.** Maslow believes that mentally healthy people are naturally curious and demonstrate this attribute through a search for meaning, culminating in "a desire to understand, to systematize, to organize, to analyze, to look for relations and meanings, to construct a system of values." **187** You will notice this type of knowledge is at the higher levels of Bloom's Taxonomy of Learning - analysis, synthesis and evaluation.

The other preoccupation of self-actualized individuals is their search for what Maslow calls the **aesthetic** and Aristotle calls **pleasures of the mind**. Maslow also believes that the need for beauty, like the quest for knowledge, is instinctive. Who doesn't appreciate a beautiful sunset or sunrise? The pioneers certainly did. Remember the lesson(seven) on the search for the aesthetic.

Both the philosopher(Aristotle) and the professor(Maslow) realize these two highest strivings of mankind are the essential components of self-actualization. The acquiring of knowledge of all sorts, together with the satisfaction derived from seeing beauty in art and Nature, are necessary for the "good life."

How do you acquire the type of knowledge that ultimately leads to wisdom in the self-actualized person? One answer is found in the first four chapters of the Book of Proverbs. Solomon concludes, "The first step is to trust and reverence the Lord" and "determination to be wise is the first step toward becoming wise." **188**

From where does beauty originate? The first chapter of Genesis describes the creation of the heavens and the earth. This natural beauty is evident all around us. "America the Beautiful" describes it well - with our fruited plains, purple mountains and shining seas. The pioneers who settled by the Pacific Ocean saw all three of these natural wonders.

Even though it's possible for an individual to become self-actualized through her/his own strength and efforts, I believe a more effective way is through tapping into a power greater than yourself. Jesus Christ's purpose on earth was "to give life in all its fullness. . . to all who received Him(humbly asked for this source of power for their own lives). **189** He was the ultimate example of a self-actualized person who still depended upon His Father for strength and guidance. If He needed this outside assistance, how much more do we in our daily strivings.

Metaneeds

As you can see by the above descriptions, self-actualizing(SA) individuals are not the "run-of-the-mill-persons" you meet on the street. Their basic needs are either satisfied or no longer important to living a fulfilled life. History records cases of martyrs sacrificing everything for a cause greater than themselves. Others deliberately lead a life of voluntary simplicity. SAs are driven by a mission or calling, and they feel intrinsically compelled to accomplish it. No one has to "make" them do it. Their "I want to" coincides with "I must." **190**

Maslow has identified 16 possible "being"(B) values to which SAs devote their lives. These B-values are what motivates these growing individuals. Diagram 9 lists these needs in the upper part of the trapezoid. They are essential for a meaningful life. Maslow also sees these B-values as fulfilling mankind's religious functions - the search for absolute and eternal verities. **191** Maybe Christ had these metaneeds in mind when he stated his purpose was "to give life in all its fullness." **192** ABRAHAM MASLOW'S HIERARCHY OF NEEDS

Diagram 9

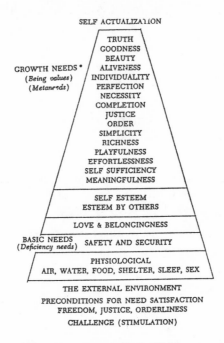

SELF ACTUALIZATION

GROWTH NEEDS *
(*Being values*)
(*Metaneeds*)

TRUTH
GOODNESS
BEAUTY
ALIVENESS
INDIVIDUALITY
PERFECTION
NECESSITY
COMPLETION
JUSTICE
ORDER
SIMPLICITY
RICHNESS
PLAYFULNESS
EFFORTLESSNESS
SELF SUFFICIENCY
MEANINGFULNESS

SELF ESTEEM
ESTEEM BY OTHERS

LOVE & BELONGINGNESS

BASIC NEEDS
(*Deficiency needs*)   SAFETY AND SECURITY

PHYSIOLOGICAL
AIR, WATER, FOOD, SHELTER, SLEEP, SEX

THE EXTERNAL ENVIRONMENT
PRECONDITIONS FOR NEED SATISFACTION
FREEDOM, JUSTICE, ORDERLINESS
CHALLENGE (STIMULATION)

* Growth needs are all of equal importance (not hierarchical)
From Goble, The Third Force, 1970, 50.

We can think of examples of persons who devote their lives to one of these metaneeds. Philosophers and theologians search for **truth**. Artists find **beauty** in their works. Martin Luther King literally gave his life for justice. Mohandas Gandhi and Mother Teresa saw **simplicity** as their mission. Mathematicians and scientists see **order** in the universe. Dramatists use the stage to demonstrate **aliveness**. Survivalists relish **self sufficiency.** All these individuals have the search for **meaning** as their raison d'etre - reason for existence.

Do you think some of the self-actualizing pioneers

devoted their lives to some of these metaneeds? Were they willing to die for any of them? We can only speculate again. After meeting their basic needs in the Willamette Valley, some settlers may have been so taken by the natural **beauty** that they became artists. Others may have deliberately lived a life of **simplicity.** A few may have worked for social **justice** in making sure the Oregon Territory came under the jurisdiction of the United States.

What about you? What values are you willing to live and die for? We would probably give our life for our family; i.e., run in front of a car to save our child. Are we willing to die for our faith? our country? anything else? Only when we know what we will die for are we ready to live. Jesus expresses this seeming paradox, "Whoever clings to his life shall lose it, and whoever loses his life shall save it." **193**

Were The Overlanders Satisfied To Stay In Oregon?

Arriving in Oregon City marked the achievement of a long-sought and arduous goal. This feat surely gave the pioneers a great deal of satisfaction. Unruh concludes his book, "It is no wonder that those who completed the adventure wrote and spoke about it often in subsequent years. It **was** something to be proud of: to have traveled the "plains across." **194**

However, after the "glow" of attainment dies down, there may be a tendency to settle into the complacency of the status quo. We know by genealogical studies in Oregon that many pioneers stayed where they settled. Today it is an honor in Oregon to be descended from a pioneer family! They evidently found and lived the "good life." They could exclaim with Marcus Whitman who wrote, "I am satisfied." **195** The Biblical command, "Be satisfied with what you have" would apply to these true settlers. **196**

We know some emigrants originally traveled West because of a spirit of restlessness(see Lesson One). Once they arrived in Oregon did they stay? Or did they again get "itchy feet" and head for "greener pastures?" Were they the ones that climbed mountains - because they were there?

Maslow sees humans as always desiring something. That is why his hierarchy presupposes a new need emerging after a lower need is satisfied. We "rarely reach a state of complete satisfaction except for a short time"[after achieving a goal]. **197**

So we see examples of the creative tension between **satisfaction** and **growth** - between admonitions from the Bible and Maslow's view. Are they compatible? I believe they are. We can be temporarily satisfied and thank God for our situation. The Apostle Paul challenges us to be content in whatever state we are in. **198** At the same time we can formulate new goals to achieve. Remember self-actualization is a lifelong process. Hopefully you can balance these two human tendencies on your journey.

Throughout these lessons you have been drawing comparisons with the pioneers. You have been answering the question, **"How am I like the pioneers?"** The next section will provide a framework to assist you in answering this application question. Your journey concludes with this summary.

Conclusion

HOW AM I LIKE THE PIONEERS?

The previous ten lessons have focused on certain aspects of the pioneers' journey along the Oregon Trail. I used lessons instead of chapters to emphasize that we could learn from their experiences. It's now time for the test - to compare their journey with ours.

The following procedure will synthesize the previous lessons and allow you to evaluate your journey vis-a-vis the emigrants' trek. You will be thinking at the higher levels of Bloom's Taxonomy of Learning(analysis, synthesis and evaluation). For each lesson, I will depict two continuums - one to rank the "**Great Emigration of 1843,**" and one to rank **yourself.** I will select one important variable from each lesson, together with two opposing values. I will use the 0-10 numerical scale to rank the pioneers on their continuum. After explaining this ranking, you may then use your continuum to rank yourself using the same variable. The higher your number, the closer you are to the "pioneer spirit." After all ten lessons have been analyzed, you can compare your total score with that of the pioneers. Have fun!

Lesson One Risk-taking: The Decision To Travel To Oregon

Pioneers' Degree of Risk

0	1	2	3	4	5	6	7	8	9	10
Status Quo										Calculated

I gave the 1843 pioneers a ranking of **9.** The decision to make the long journey qualifies them as calculated risk-takers. For nine of ten emigrants, the risk paid off. However, they prepared themselves with supplies to try to minimize possible problems. But their success was not a certainty. Still they launched into mostly unfamiliar territory to seek their "good life."

Your Degree of Risk

0	1	2	3	4	5	6	7	8	9	10
Status Quo										Calculated

How much of a risk-taker are you? Are you willing to change with the times?

Your Ranking: ____

Your Reasoning:

Lesson Two Supplies: Knowing What To Take

Pioneers' Type of Supplies

0	1	2	3	4	5	6	7	8	9	10
Wants										Needs

I gave the pioneers a ranking of **8.** They basically brought provisions that would satisfy Maslow's physiological level needs(similar to Aristotle's physical goods). As the journey progressed and the animals tired of pulling heavy loads, those nonessential items that could be discarded along the Trail became apparent - and not real - goods. These wants contributed to the greatest "litterbugging" in American history.

How about you? How many of your possessions would you classify as needs? wants? Use the following continuum to rank your answer.

Your Possessions

0	1	2	3	4	5	6	7	8	9	10
Wants										Needs

How many of your possessions would you classify as needs? as wants?

Your Ranking: _____

Your Reasoning:

Lesson Three Guides and Guidebooks: Finding The Way

Pioneers' Reliability of Information

0	1	2	3	4	5	6	7	8	9	10
Low										High

I ranked this variable as a **2**. The emigrants, especially those traveling in the 1840s, had little reliable information on which to base their decisions. Their guidebooks and maps were sketchy, often relying on conflicting personal accounts of fur trappers and early explorers. The wagon masters probably didn't use a systematic decision-making process to decide which route to take. They made a decision and hoped the Trail would eventually lead them to the "Promised Land." There were no Rand McNally atlantes or AAA services to plot the most efficient route.

Your Reliability of Information

0	1	2	3	4	5	6	7	8	9	10
Low										High

How accurate is the information you receive from various media sources? Do you use this information to make rational decisions?

Your Ranking: ___

Your Reasoning:

Lesson Four Water: Lifeblood Of The Journey

Pioneers' Appreciation of Water

0	1	2	3	4	5	6	7	8	9	10
Low										High

Here the pioneers ranked a **9.**   The search for water was their most important preoccupation along the Trail. Its availability determined their route and nightly campsites. The wagon trains rarely strayed from rivers, falls and springs. Even though they may have polluted the rivers and acquired cholera from the lack of sanitary facilities(no sewage treatment plants then!), water made the journey successful for the overwhelming majority of emigrants.

Your Appreciation of Water

0	1	2	3	4	5	6	7	8	9	10
Low										High

How important is water to you in your everyday routine? What measures do you take to conserve water?

Your Ranking(may depend on how plentiful the water supply is in your region of the United States)

Your Reasoning:

Lesson Five Forts and Missions: Oases On The Plains

Pioneers' Degree of Protection

0	1	2	3	4	5	6	7	8	9	10
Vulnerable										Safe

This ranking of **5** represents the pioneers' relative safety on the entire Trail. They were obviously more vulnerable on the open prairie to adverse weather and unfriendly Indians. However, once they reached a fort, its stockaded wall furnished welcome protection. These rare refuges also provided time for rest, restoration and relaxation - time to renew themselves physically, socially and spiritually.

Your Degree of Protection

0	1	2	3	4	5	6	7	8	9	10
Vulnerable										Safe

How safe do you feel today? How much time do you take for rest, restoration and relaxation?

Your Ranking: __

Your Reasoning:

Lesson Six Landmarks: Enjoying The Aesthetic Beauty

Pioneers' Appreciation of the Natural Beauty

0	1	2	3	4	5	6	7	8	9	10
Low										High

Here the pioneers score a **9**. Their entire journey was surrounded by natural beauty and landmarks. They were always outside(except for brief stays in forts and missions), and lumbered along slowly. These two factors would allow men, women and children to appreciate the trees, bluffs, rock formations, hills and mountains.

Your Appreciation of the Natural Beauty

0	1	2	3	4	5	6	7	8	9	10
Low										High

Do you take time to "smell the flowers" along the way? Do you spend time enjoying the majestic beauty of the great outdoors? Do you reflect upon the landmarks in your life?

Your Ranking: ___

Your Reasoning:

Lesson Seven Weather: Preparing For The Changes

Pioneers' Degree of Change

0	1	2	3	4	5	6	7	8	9	10
Rigid										Flexible

The emigrants' flexibility is shown by a ranking of **8**. The overlanders no doubt established daily travel goals. Under ideal conditions they may have traveled twenty miles. However, they had to adapt to frightening thunderstorms, wind-swept dust storms and possible snowstorms and blizzards in the mountains. In these situations they went to Plan B and vowed to achieve a loftier goal the next day.

Your Degree of Change

0	1	2	3	4	5	6	7	8	9	10
Rigid										Flexible

How do you deal with plans gone awry? Does it have to be your way or else? Do you have a Plan B, or C if needed?

Your Ranking: ___

Your Reasoning:

Lesson Eight Family, Friends and Indians: Depending Upon Each Other

Pioneers' Importance of Friendship

0	1	2	3	4	5	6	7	8	9	10
Many Acquaintances						Few Close Friends				

This ranking is at the midpoint - **5.** The pioneers left their old friends and relatives back East before embarking to Oregon. However, they met new people on the Trail. Some were merely acquaintances, enjoying "small talk" to wile away the time on the long journey. Some probably became friends in whom they could confide by sharing their personal life. In any case the persons in the wagon train could be depended upon to share the daily tasks and pull together during a crisis.

Importance of Friendship to You

0	1	2	3	4	5	6	7	8	9	10

Many acquaintances   Few Close Friends

Do you have many acquaintances or a few close friends with which to share your life? Which type is more important to you?

Your Ranking: ___

Your Reasoning:

Lesson Nine Practicing Discipline and Overcoming Obstacles: Producing Character

Pioneers' Success in Overcoming Obstacles

0	1	2	3	4	5	6	7	8	**9**	10

Succumber   Overcomer

This ranking is a resounding **9** - for the approximately ninety percent who finished the journey! These survivors conquered disease, death, hostile Indians, physical exhaustion and mental monotony. Their discipline proved the slogan, "When the going gets tough, the tough gets going."

Your Success in Overcoming Obstacles

0	1	2	3	4	5	6	7	8	9	10

Succumber   Overcomer

How do you handle hardships in your life? Do you see problems as barriers or challenges? Defeats or opportunities?

Your Ranking: ___

Your Reasoning:

Lesson Ten Achieving The Goal: Arriving In Oregon City

Pioneers and Self-Actualization

0	1	2	3	4	5	6	7	8	9	10
Lower Level Needs							Self-Actualization			

This final ranking merits a **9**. The emigrants' "good life" goal was finally reached in Oregon. Their journey was complete! However, as Maslow explains, self-actualization is an ongoing process - you never really arrive. The settlers could now concentrate on reaching their potential in the lush Willamette Valley.

Self-Actualization and You

0	1	2	3	4	5	6	7	8	9	10
Lower Level Needs							Self-Actualization			

Where are you on your life's "journey?" How close are you to becoming all you can become?

Your Ranking: ___

Your Reasoning:

The Pioneers and You

Now that you have ranked the pioneers and yourself vis-a-vis ten lessons, its time to compare the results. How do you stack up with these adventurers?

Composite Pioneer Rankings
(total of above ten continuums): **73**

Composite Rankings For Yourself: ___

If your score is equal or above **73**, you qualify as a pioneer! How did you do?

150 years later we still refer to the "pioneer spirit." Hopefully these lessons will assist you in rekindling their indomitable traits as you journey through life. May these courageous emigrants be with you! See you on the Trail!

ENDNOTES

Introduction

1   William E. Hill, **The Oregon Trail: Yesterday and Today**, Caldwell, Idaho, The Caxton Printers, Ltd., 1987, xxv.

Lesson One Risk-Taking

2   John Naisbitt, **Megatrends: Ten New Directions Transforming Our Lives**, New York, Warner Books, 1982, 208.
3   Ibid., 215.
4   **The World Almanac And Book Of Facts: 1992**, New York, Pharos Books, 1991, 72.
5   Naisbitt, 210-11.
6   Charles R. Swindoll, **Abraham: A Model Of Pioneer Faith**, Anaheim, California, Insight for Living, 1992, 2.
7   Ibid., 19.
8   Ibid., 20.
9   Ibid., 21.
10 Ibid.
11 Ibid., 22.
12 David Lavender, **Westward Vision: The Story of the Oregon Trail**, Lincoln, Nebraska, University of Nebraska Press, 1963, 347.
13 Richard Nelson Bolles, **What Color Is Your Parachute? A Practical Manual for Job Hunters & Career Changers**, Berkeley, California, Ten Speed Press, 1989, 348-49.
14 Ibid., 358.
15 Ibid., 362.
16 Swindoll, 22.

Lesson Two Supplies

17 W. J. Ghent, **Road to Oregon**, New York, Longmans Green and Company, 1929, 100.
18 **The Living Bible**, Wheaton, Illinois, Tyndale House Publishers, 1971, 1903(Romans 7:15).
19 Mortimer J. Adler, **Aristotle For Everybody: Difficult Thought Made Easy**, New York, Macmillan Publishing Co., Inc., 88.
20 Ibid., 90.

21 Richard McKeon, ed., **Introduction to Aristotle**, "Ethics," New York, Random House, Inc., 1947, 357.

22 **The Living Bible**, 481(Psalm 90:12).

23 Charles Hummel, "Tyranny of the Urgent," Champaign-Urbana, Illinois, Inter-Varsity Press.

24 Gordon MacDonald, **Ordering Your Private World**, Nashville, Tennessee, Oliver-Nelson, 1985, 72.

25 **The Living Bible**, 451(Psalm 19: 1-6), 469(Psalms 65: 6-13), 485(Psalm 104: 1-28).

Lesson Three Guides and Guidebooks

26 David Lavender, **The Overland Migrations**, Washington, D. C., Division of Publications, National Park Service, U. S. Department of the Interior, 44.

27 Lavender, **Westward Vision,** 369.

28 Hill, xxvii.

29 Lavender, **Westward Vision,** 366-67.

30 Naisbitt, 24.

31 Aubrey L. Haines, **Historic Sites Along THE OREGON TRAIL**, St. Louis,   The Patrice Press, 1981, 242.

32 Ibid, 366.

33 Janice Castro, "The Simple Life," **Time**, April 8, 1991, 58.

34 **The Living Bible**, 750(Matthew 7: 13, 14).

35 Ibid., 867(Acts 5: 29).

36 Robert Frost, **Complete Poems of Robert Frost**, New York, Holt, Rinehart, and Winston, Inc., 1949, 131.

Lesson Four Water

37 **The Living Bible**, 460-61(Psalms 42: 1-2).

38 Ibid., 840(John 4: 13-14).

39 John D. Unruh, Jr., **The Plains Across: The Overland Emigrants and the Trans-Mississippi West, 1840-60**, Chicago, University of Illinois Press, 1979, 326-27.

40 Haines, 39.

41 Ibid., 76.

42 Ibid., 182.

43 Ibid., 205.

44 Ibid., 328.

45 Ibid., 342.

46 Ibid., 45-46.

47 Ibid., 285.

48 Ibid., 329.

49 Ibid., 346.

50 Ibid., 326.

51 Ibid., 221-22.

52 Marvin Cetron and Thomas O'Toole, **Encounters with the Future: A Forecast of Life into the 21st Century**, St. Louis, McGraw-Hill, 1982, 34.

53 Richard Boyer & David Savageau, **Places Rated Almanac: Your Guide to Finding the Best Places to Live in America**, New York, Prentice Hall Travel, 1989, 382.

54 Ibid., 381.

55 Ibid., 34.

56 **The Living Bible**, 441-42(Job 36: 22 - 37: 18).

Lesson Five Forts and Missions

57 Haines, 60.

58 Ibid., 136.

59 Ibid., 135.

60 Ibid., 272.

61 Ibid., 297.

62 Ibid., 339.

63 Ibid., 371.

64 Ibid., 405-6.

65 Ibid., 30.

66 Ibid., 42.

67 Ibid., 381.

68 **The World Almanac and Book of Facts: 1992**, 954.

69 **The Living Bible**, 275(II Samuel 22: 2).

70 Ibid., 450(Psalms 18: 2) and 500(Psalms 144: 2).

71 **The Christian Science Monitor**, December 21, 1990, 19.

72 Ibid., March 18, 1991, 14.

73 Ibid., December 21, 1990.

74 MacDonald, 165.

75 Ibid., 167.

Lesson Six Landmarks

76 Haines, 33.

77 Ibid., 54.

78 Ibid., 90.

79 Ibid., 351.

80 Stephen R. Covey, **The Seven Habits of Highly Effective People: Restoring the Character Ethic**, New York, Simon and Schuster, 1989, 54.

81 **The Living Bible**, 481(Psalms 92: 12).

82 Robert Cortes Holliday, ed., **Joyce Kilmer: Memoir and Poems**, Volume 1, New York, Doubleday and Co., Inc., 1946, 180.

83 Harold S. Kushner, **When All You've Ever Wanted Isn't Enough**, New York, Summit Books, 1986, 20.

84 Ibid., 172.

85 Haines, 93.

86 "Chimney Rock," Washington, D. C., National Park Service, Department of the Interior, 1.

87 Haines, 197.

88 Charles W. Martin and Charles W. Martin, Jr., "The Fourth of July: A Holiday on the Trail," **Overland Journal**, Volume 10, Number 2, Summer, 1992, 3, 15.

89 Haines, 198.

90 Ibid., 207.

91 Ibid., 313-14.

92 Ibid., 36-37.

93 Ibid., 401, 403.

94 **The Living Bible**, 1(Genesis 1: 27).

95 Emmie Bohm, "My Mountain Home," poem furnished by Marvieu Mennenga, Belmond, Iowa.

96 Haines, 169.

97 **The Living Bible**, 462(Psalms 46: 10).

Lesson Seven Weather

98 Ibid., 751(Matthew 7: 26-27).

99 Boyer and Savageau, 323.

100 Unruh, 322.

101 Lavender, **The Overland Migrations**, 54.

102 Boyer and Savageau, 340, 354.

103 Lavender, **The Overland Migrations**, 65.

104 Unruh, 311.

105 Ibid., 299.

106 Boyer and Savageau, 325-26.

107 Barbara Clark, **Growing Up Gifted: Developing the Potential of Children at Home and at School**, second edition, Columbus, Ohio, Charles E. Merrill Publishing Company, 1983, 311.

108 **The Living Bible**, 424(Job 1: 21, 2: 10).

Lesson Eight   Family, Friends and Indians

109 Naisbitt, 232-33.

110 **The Des Moines Register**, November 1, 1992, 3E.

111 Covey, 150-52.

112 Ibid.

113 Unruh, 85.

114 Ibid., 94.

115 Ibid., 106, 108, 110.

116 Ibid., 100-02.

117 Ibid., 103, 105-06.

118 Ibid., 87-89.

119 Ibid., 94-100.

120 Ibid., 103-05.

121 **World Almanac and Book of Facts: 1992**, 73.

122 Naisbitt, 39.

123 **World Almanac and Book of Facts: 1992**, 317-18.

124 McKeon, 471,511.

125 **The Living Bible**, 525(Ecclesiastes 4: 9).

126 McKeon, 475.

127 **The Living Bible**, 945(Galatians 5: 22).

128 McKeon, 518.

129 Ibid., 479, 514.

130 **The Living Bible**, 519(Proverbs 27: 17).

131 Lavender, **The Overland Migrations**, 49.

132 Unruh, 140-41.

133 Ibid., 144, 155.

134 Ibid., 118.

135 Ibid., 119-20, 125.

136 Ibid., 124, 126.

137 Ibid., 158.

Lesson Nine
   Practicing Discipline And Overcoming Obstacles

138 Webster's Seventh New Collegiate Dictionary, Springfield, Massachusetts, G. & C. Merriam Company, 1965, 237.

139 Ghent, 73-75.

140 Ibid., 75-76.

141 M. Scott Peck, The Road Less Traveled: A New Psychology of Love, Traditional Values and Spiritual Growth, New York, Simon and Schuster, 1978, 15.

142 The Living Bible, 986(James 1: 2).

143 Peck, 15.

144 Ibid., 19.

145 The Living Bible, 750(Matthew 7: 13).

146 The Christian Science Monitor, December 18, 1992, 8.

147 The Living Bible, 66(Exodus 20: 14), 917(I Corinthians 6: 13), 946(Galatians 6: 7).

148 Charles Lester, Redeemer Lutheran Church, Des Moines, Iowa.

149 Viktor E. Frankl, Man's Search For Meaning, New York, Washington Square Press, 1984, 86.

150 The Living Bible, 834(Luke 23: 34).

151 Ibid., 859(Luke 18: 38).

152 Ibid., 854(John 14: 6), 846-47(John 8: 32).

153 Webster's Seventh New Collegiate Dictionary, 953.

154 Covey, 277.

155 Peck, 51.

156 Ibid., 63.

157 Ibid., 64.

158 "All Things Considered," National Public Radio, January 14, 1993.

159 McKeon, 347.

160 Covey, 304.

161 The Living Bible, 803(Luke 2: 52).

162 Richard L. Rieck, "A Geography of Death on the Oregon-California Trail, 1840-1860, " Overland Journal, Volume 9, Number 1, Spring, 1991, 14.

163 Unruh, 345.

164 David E. Larson, M.D., Editor-In-Chief, Mayo Clinic Family Health Book, New York, William Morrow and Company, Inc., 1990, 306.

165 Rieck, 14.

166 Unruh, 346.

167 Ibid., 346-47.

168 Rieck, 15-16.

169 Unruh, 347.

170 Ibid., 348-49.

171 Hill, xxxi.

172 Ibid., xxx.

173 Ibid., xxxii.

174 Rieck, 18.

175 Ghent, 113.

176 Unruh, 350.

177 Victor Goertzel and Mildred Goertzel, **Cradles of Eminence**, Boston, Little, Brown and Company, 1962, 272.

178 **The Living Bible**, 986(James 1: 2-4).

Lesson Ten   Achieving The Goal

179 Lavender, **The Overland Migrations**, 46.

180 Ralph Waldo Emerson, "Success," furnished by Dennis Flood, Omaha, Nebraska.

181 Frank G. Goble, **The Third Force: The Psychology of Abraham Maslow**, New York, Grossman Publishers, 1970, 41.

182 Ibid.

183 Ibid., 24-25.

184 Abraham H. Maslow, **Toward A Psychology of Being**, 2nd ed., Cincinnati, Van Nostrand Reinhold Company, 1968, 25.

185 Goble, 25-34, Maslow, 26 and Maslow, **The Farther Reaches of Human Nature**, New York, The Viking Press, 1971, 45-49.

186 Maslow, **The Farther Reaches of Human Nature**, 45 and 50.

187 Goble, 33.

188 **The Living Bible**, 502(Proverbs 1: 7) and 504(Proverbs 4: 7).

189 Ibid., 849(John 10: 10) and 836(John 1: 12).

190 Maslow, **The Farther Reaches of Human Nature**, 302.

191 Ibid., 43-44 and 339.

192 **The Living Bible**, 849(John 10: 10).

193 Ibid., 825(Luke 17: 33).

194 Unruh, 352.

195 Lavender, **Westward Vision**, 381.

196 **The Living Bible**, 985(Hebrews 13: 5).

197 Goble, 38.

198 **The Living Bible**, 955(Philippians 4: 11-12).

BIBLIOGRAPHY

Books

Adler, Mortimer J., **Aristotle For Everybody: Difficult Thought Made Easy**. New York: Macmillan Publishing Co., Inc., 1978.

Bolles, Richard Nelson. **What Color Is Your Parachute? A Practical Manual for Job Hunters & Career Changers**. Berkeley, California, Ten Speed Press, 1989.

Boyer, Richard & David Savageau. **Places Rated Almanac: Your Guide to Finding the Best Places to Live in America**. New York: Prentice Hall Travel, 1989.

Cetron, Marvin and Thomas O'Toole. **Encounters with the Future: A Forecast of Life into the 21st Century**. St. Louis: McGraw-Hill Book Company, 1982.

Clark, Barbara. **Growing Up Gifted: Developing the Potential of Children at Home and at School**, second edition. Columbus, Ohio: Charles E. Merrill Publishing Company, 1983.

Covey, Stephen R. **The Seven Habits of Highly Effective People: Restoring the Character Ethic**. New York: Simon and Schuster, 1989.

Frankl, Viktor E. **Man's Search For Meaning**. New York: Washington Square Press, 1984.

Frost, Robert. **Complete Poems of Robert Frost**. New York: Holt, Rinehart, and Winston, Inc., 1949.

Ghent, W. J. **Road to Oregon**. New York: Longmans Green and Company, 1929.

Goble, Frank G. **The Third Force: The Psychology of Abraham Maslow**. New York: Grossman Publishers, 1970.

Goertzel, Victor and Mildred Goertzel. **Cradles of Eminence**. Boston: Little, Brown and Company, 1962.

Haines, Aubrey. **Historic Sites Along THE OREGON TRAIL**. St. Louis: The Patrice Press, 1981.

Heat Moon, William Least. **Blue Highways: A Journey Into America**. Boston: Little, Brown and Company, 1982.

Hill, William E. **The Oregon Trail: Yesterday and Today**. Caldwell, Idaho: The Caxton Printers, Ltd., 1987.

Holliday, Robert Cortes, ed. **Joyce Kilmer: Memoir and Poems,** Volume 1. New York: Doubleday and Co., Inc., 1946.

Kushner, Harold S. **When All You've Ever Wanted Isn't Enough.** New York: Summit Books, 1986.

Larson, David E., M.D., Editor-In-Chief, **Mayo Clinic Family Health Book.** New York: William Morrow and Company, Inc., 1990.

Lavender, David. **The Overland Migrations.** Washington, D. C., Division of Publications, National Park Service, U. S. Department of Interior.

Lavender, David. **Westward Vision: The Story of the Oregon Trail.** Lincoln, Nebraska: University of Nebraska Press, 1963.

The Living Bible. Wheaton, Illinois: Tyndale House Publishers, Inc., 1971.

MacDonald, Gordon. **Ordering Your Private World.** Nashville, Tennessee: Oliver-Nelson, 1985.

Maslow, Abraham H. **The Farther Reaches of Human Nature.** New York: The Viking Press, 1971.

Maslow, Abraham H. **Toward A Psychology of Being,** 2nd ed., Cincinnati: Van Nostrand Reinhold Company, 1968.

McKeon, Richard, ed. **Introduction to Aristotle.** New York: Random House, Inc., 1947.

Naisbitt, John. **Megatrends: Ten Directions Transforming Our Lives.** New York: Warner Books, 1982.

Peck, M. Scott. **The Road Less Traveled: A New Psychology of Love, Traditional Values and Spiritual Growth.** New York: Simon and Schuster, 1978.

Porter, Burton. **The Good Life: Alternatives In Ethics.** New York: Macmillan Publishing Company, Inc., 1980.

Swindoll, Charles R. **Abraham: A Model Of Pioneer Faith.** Anaheim, California: Insight for Living, 1992.

Unruh, John D., Jr. **The Plains Across: The Overland Emigrants and the Trans-Mississippi West, 1840-60.** Chicago: University of Illinois Press, 1982.

Webster's Seventh New Collegiate Dictionary. Springfield, Massachusetts: G. & C. Merriam Company, 1965.

The World Almanac And Book Of Facts: 1992. New York: Pharos Books, 1991.

Periodicals

Castro, Janice, "The Simple Life," Time, April 8, 1991, 58-63.

"Chimney Rock," Washington, D. C., National Park Service, Department of the Interior, 1-6.

The Christian Science Monitor, December 21, 1990, 19.

The Christian Science Monitor, March 18, 1991, 14.

The Christian Science Monitor, December 18, 1992, 8.

The Des Moines Register, November 1, 1992, 3E.

Hummel, Charles, "Tyranny of the Urgent," Champaign-Urbana, Illinois, Inter-Varsity Press.

Martin, Charles W. and Charles W. Martin, Jr., "The Fourth of July: A Holiday on the Trail,"Overland Journal, Volume 10, Number 2, Summer, 1992, 2-20.

Rieck, Richard L., "A Geography of Death on the Oregon-California Trail, 1840-1860," Overland Journal, Volume 9, Number 1, Spring, 1991, 13-21.

Other Sources

"All Things Considered," National Public Radio, January 14, 1993.

Barker, Joel, "The Power of Vision."

Discher, Ken, Grimes, Iowa, revised Diagram 2.

Flood, Dennis, Omaha, Nebraska, furnished Ralph Waldo Emerson's prose "Success."

Lester, Charles, Redeemer Lutheran Church, Des Moines, Iowa.

Mennenga, Marvieu, furnished Emmie Bohm's poem"My Mountain Home"

INDEX Of Historic Sites Along The Oregon Trail

MULTIPLE INTELLIGENCES PROFILE INDICATOR

PLEASE INDICATE FOR THE FOLLOWING ITEMS THE DEGREE TO WHICH YOU THINK THE STATED
CHARACTERISTIC OR BEHAVIOR FITS THE INDIVIDUAL IN QUESTION. CIRCLE THE APPROPRIATE
NUMBER:

0 = Unsure   1 = Fits not at all   2 = Fits slightly   3 = Fits moderately   4 = Fits strongly

This individual:

1. Likes to identify or create categories and to sort objects or
    ideas into categories.   0 1 2 3 4

2. Is physically very active but generally in very purposeful ways.   0 1 2 3 4

3. Draws a lot; uses diagrams, sketches, or pictures to help
    explain or understand ideas and feelings.   0 1 2 3 4

4. Able to express accurately his/her inner feelings or
    self-knowledge in a variety of ways.   0 1 2 3 4

5. Learns to put together complex sequences of physical
    activities or routines with relative ease.   0 1 2 3 4

6. Able to follow complex lines of reasoning.   0 1 2 3 4

7. Likes to read, write, or talk a lot.   0 1 2 3 4

8. Acts on the basis of knowledge of self.   0 1 2 3 4

9. Likes to act out things, to show physically how something
    works or can be done.   0 1 2 3 4

10. Can figure out how to do fairly complex things just by
    observing the process or looking at picture or diagrams.   0 1 2 3 4

11. Very sensitive to the meanings of words and tends to choose
    words for their exactness or precision.   0 1 2 3 4

12. Seeks interaction with others; enjoys the challenge of
    interacting with others.   0 1 2 3 4

13. Easily creates mental images of things and ideas; is able
    easily to change or modify mental images of things.   0 1 2 3 4

14. Very sensitive to rhythm, pitch, and qualities of tone in music.   0 1 2 3 4

Developed by Frank Rainey, State Consultant for Gifted and Talented,
Colorado Department of Education

15. Likes to build things, take things apart, put things together; may take something apart and put it together again so it is different from the way it was originally. 0 1 2 3 4

16. Very sensitive to the effect words have on himself/herself or others when reading, writing, or speaking. 0 1 2 3 4

17. Likes to discuss or argue ideas; enjoys finding holes or filling gaps in logical reasoning. 0 1 2 3 4

18. Understands his/her own inner feelings, motivations, and intentions. 0 1 2 3 4

19. Gets along well with others; is likeable and sociable. 0 1 2 3 4

20. Likes to listen to music or to perform music. 0 1 2 3 4

21. Recognizes patterns and relationships among objects and ideas. 0 1 2 3 4

22. Likes to experiment with things in controlled, orderly ways. 0 1 2 3 4

23. Very sensitive to the effect music has on himself/herself or on others. 0 1 2 3 4

24. Able to figure out the way something is done or works or how something is constructed simply by studying the finished product. 0 1 2 3 4

25. Can use his/her hands and fingers with great skill and control. 0 1 2 3 4

26. Likes puns, word games, and other humor with words and language. 0 1 2 3 4

27. Economical in the use of body movements. 0 1 2 3 4

28. Very sensitive to the feelings and moods of others. 0 1 2 3 4

29. Individualistic; not unduly concerned about what others might think about him or her. 0 1 2 3 4

30. Often able to figure out the motivations and intentions of others; able to act using knowledge of others. 0 1 2 3 4

31. Has a large vocabulary; likes to use or experiment with new or sophisticated words. 0 1 2 3 4

32. Independent and generally self-assured. 0 1 2 3 4

Developed by Frank Rainey, State Consultant for Gifted and Talented
Colorado Department of Education

33.	Likes to make up tunes or melodies.	0 1 2 3 4
34.	Senses musical elements (rhythm, pitch, and qualities of tone) in situations not generally associated with music.	0 1 2 3 4
35.	Able to influence others; persuasive.	0 1 2 3 4
36.	Has a good sense of timing in physical activities.	0 1 2 3 4
37.	Has a strong and accurate inner sense of what he or she wants or needs.	0 1 2 3 4
38.	Reads body language well.	0 1 2 3 4
39.	Able to devise orderly systems or plans for accomplishing complex tasks.	0 1 2 3 4
40.	Likes to improvise with music.	0 1 2 3 4
41.	Uses language skillfully to explain things or to show how conclusions have been drawn.	0 1 2 3 4
42.	Has a strong sense of composition in art, photography, or interior decorating.	0 1 2 3 4

Developed by Frank Rainey, State Consultant for Gifted and Talented
Colorado Department of Education

DIRECTIONS FOR SCORING

1. Transfer response values from pages 1-3 to matching item number on this page. Use Column A.

	A	B	C
LINGUISTIC			
7.	_____	_____	
11.	_____	_____	
16.	_____	_____	
26.	_____	_____	
31.	_____	_____	
41.	_____	_____	_____
	A	B	C
LOGICAL/MATHEMATICAL			
1.	_____	_____	
6.	_____	_____	
17.	_____	_____	
21.	_____	_____	
22.	_____	_____	
39.	_____	_____	_____
	A	B	C
BODILY/KINESTHETIC			
2.	_____	_____	
5.	_____	_____	
9.	_____	_____	
25.	_____	_____	
27.	_____	_____	
36.	_____	_____	_____
	A	B	C
INTRAPERSONAL			
4.	_____	_____	
8.	_____	_____	
18.	_____	_____	
29.	_____	_____	
32.	_____	_____	
37.	_____	_____	_____
	A	B	C

	A	B	C
MUSICAL			
14.	_____	_____	
20.	_____	_____	
23.	_____	_____	
33.	_____	_____	
34.	_____	_____	
40.	_____	_____	_____
	A	B	C
SPATIAL			
3.	_____	_____	
10.	_____	_____	
13.	_____	_____	
15.	_____	_____	
24.	_____	_____	
42.	_____	_____	_____
	A	B	C
INTERPERSONAL			
12.	_____	_____	
19.	_____	_____	
28.	_____	_____	
30.	_____	_____	
35.	_____	_____	
38.	_____	_____	_____
	A	B	C

2. Multiply each response value as follows and record in Column B:

    If response = 0, multiply x 0
    If response = 1, multiply x 0
    If response = 2, multiply x 1
    If response = 3, multiply x 2
    If response = 4, multiply x 3

3. In Column C, record average for Column B for each domain. Round to nearest whole.

Developed by Frank Rainey, State Consultant for Gifted and Talented
Colorado Department of Education